BECAUSE THERE ARE TWO SIDES
TO EVERY STORY

COOPER

——— CHRONICLES OF ———
A FOUR-LEGGED FOODIE

KRISTIN PURTELL

ABOUT THE AUTHOR

Kristin Purtell is a first-time author and avid Cubs fan. She is self-employed and lives in the Chicagoland area with her husband, Steve; their two children, Madison and Alex; Cooper, and their new rescue puppy, Ernie (as in Ernie Banks).

For Steve, Madison, Alex and most of all Cooper—
FINALLY giving him a voice to explain what really
happened

CONTENTS

CHAPTER ONE

NEW BEGINNINGS

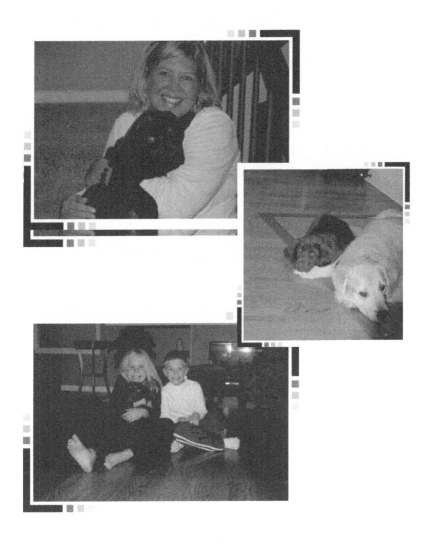

If anyone ever tells you that a golden retriever and a Labrador retriever are basically the same dog with a different hairstyle, they are greatly misinformed.

We were the typical, newly engaged couple trying to break in our relationship by adopting a dog to help us get ready for kids. Fitzroy, our new golden retriever baby, was the most perfect dog ever. Fitz didn't bark, didn't jump on people, and peed like a girl (meaning he didn't constantly "mark" his territory). The poor dog even got humped in the park regularly, despite his manly hundred-pound physique. Fast forward twelve years, and we had two healthy, vivacious, elementary school-age children, Madison and Alex, who both loved Fitzroy, and every other dog they came across.

But our "baby" was slowing down, showing signs of aging, and we would do anything to hold onto his youth. Google research claimed that introducing a puppy to the family frequently helped to keep the older dog "young," which I rationally explained to my husband, Steve. You will soon learn that "Google" is my trusted source for all important information.

Every few weeks, the kids had been asking for a new playmate for Fitzroy but until then, we had managed to resist. Each year, I always threw out the annual bribe that if the Cubs won the World Series, we would get a second dog and name him Wrigley. Fortunately, or unfortunately, that is not how this story begins.

I still blame my neighbor, Mary Beth, for the idea. During one of our morning walks after the kids were off to school, I told her I was sad about Fitzroy getting old. Mary Beth shared that a nearby local family had twelve chocolate lab puppies. She suggested we go "take a look." Let's be real, I question the heart of anyone who can just go "take a look" at twelve chocolate lab puppies and not walk out with an additional family member. I shared the idea with Steve who shockingly agreed that we surprise the kids and go take a look that night after dinner.

I'll never forget the day. Madison and Alex were watching television after homework and dinner when I asked if anyone wanted ice cream. Before I had the words out of my mouth, the kids were putting on their shoes, ready to walk to Dairy Queen. "Not walking today, guys," I said. "We have to stop and run an errand first, so we're going to drive."

"NOOOO," they shouted in unison. "Do we have to go? Can't you just bring it back? We don't want to wait while you talk to a million people we don't know!" Not exactly how I planned to start, but, then again, I was still convinced we were "just looking." Little did they know, we were headed to a magical wonderland of puppies!

As we walked into the house, the kids screamed, "Mom, look at all the puppies! Are we getting one?"

"Just looking right now, kids, but let's see if there are any we like," I replied. Which in hindsight was the most ludicrous statement I could have made. There we were, all sitting on the floor, with twelve brown, furry, bundles of joy, nine females and three males, crawling all over and smothering us in wet sloppy kisses. Each puppy had either a pink or blue collar tied around their neck with a name written on it so we could tell them apart. Charlie, as they called him, was the largest of the bunch with a box head about the size of some of his siblings' bodies, and paws rivaling my son's six-year-old fist. As much as I hate to admit it, Charlie stole my heart immediately. He was the mellowest one in the group who just did his own thing and didn't appear to be very needy. Which, by the way, is what Google told me to look for in a puppy. Other littermates—Frankie, Reece, and Desiree—were also family favorites. Two hours later, we had not only decided we were getting a dog but had narrowed it down between Frankie and Charlie. We left to think about it and would decide the next day. Needless to say, we never got ice cream that night, but no one was disappointed.

When we got home, the kids were excited. Steve and I were pretty much in shock about the life-altering event that we had just set in motion. Fitzroy was just pissed; he would've been happy with the ice cream. He walked up to all of us and smelled everyone for quite a while, then walked away pouting. Little did he know what was in his future. Whichever pup we selected would have lots to live up to— the reputation of his older, wiser brother, Fitzroy was second to none. To this day, when Madison and Alex ask who my favorite child is, I frequently answer Fitzroy.

The decision at hand was Charlie or Frankie. It was Charlie, the largest in the litter, who'd won my heart. Cuddly Frankie was the favorite of Steve, Madison, and Alex. Logically, we selected Charlie. Similar to everyday life in our household, things tend to swing my way—*Happy Wife (Mom), Happy Life*. The hard part was over, now it was time to name him. Based on the simple fact that my fathers' name is Charlie, that was out. We brainstormed over the next few days and ended up with Cooper. As we did with Fitzroy, named after Fitzroy Island in Australia, our plan was to name him after something meaningful to us. We are a family of skiers, and Copper Mountain has always been our favorite. That was the vote of Madison and Alex. However, his dark-brown, coffee color fur wasn't exactly "Copper," so we settled with Cooper. The countdown had begun. Twenty-eight days until our lives would change forever.

The puppies were only four weeks old and couldn't be taken home for four more weeks. This was perfect because Steve and I had a trip to San Francisco planned. A new puppy entering the picture was not in the agreement with my mother, who was staying with the kids while we were gone.

The day had finally come! Fitzroy was less than pleased when a ten-pound brown bundle leaped into the house and on, over, and around him, licking and not leaving him alone. He did eventually come around, and I frequently found them lying next to each other when no one was looking. I also firmly believe that getting Cooper did help to keep Fitzroy with us for a bit longer—he lived for another year and three months from the date we brought Cooper home.

Not much stood out during the first year; it was typical puppy behavior. Cooper was actually pretty well-behaved and slept in his crate every evening without complaint. Our biggest problem was stopping him from eating Fitzroy's food along with his. We had the usual shoes being snacked on, but no major catastrophes. We were beginning to think we had dodged a bullet and our lab was going to be different from all the others we had heard stories about.

But the future was yet to prove that hope wrong.

What really happened (from Cooper's perspective)

YOUR BEST IDEA YET

Journal entry from September 2009:

I know I can never live up to my older brother's reputation as "Fitzroy, the Perfect Dog," so I'll have to make do and make my own footprint in the family as "the smart one." It shouldn't be too difficult, considering that when Fitzroy was a puppy, he swallowed an entire ball in the park trying to keep it away from another dog's owner. They had to rush him for emergency surgery to remove the ball. What an idiot, and he's the "perfect" dog? I plan to focus on food, no need to waste my time on other trivial things like tennis balls. First, they don't taste great, and second, the after-effects are not pleasant. Of course, as a puppy, I will have to break in my teeth on some shoes, but it's only because I'm missing the shoe's owner, am lonely, and, frankly, a bit bored. I am also not thrilled about this whole "crate thing," as they call it.

They force me in this small metal box with bars and a lock every night to sleep, while Fitzroy gets to head upstairs to his nice, comfortable, Tempur-Pedic dog bed right next to Mom and Dad. It's just not fair. They call it a "crate." In my opinion, "torture chamber" is a much more appropriate word. I'll deal with it for a while until I grow and get a better handle on my fine motor skills, but this is NOT going to be a long-term thing.

I love my new family. Dad is fantastic with the early-morning and late-night walks. Unfortunately, he travels frequently for work, so I don't get to see as much of him as I'd like. Madison rocks. A nine-year-old fourth grader, she tries to train me but ends up just giving me treats for doing rather simple things—I've already got her pegged as the softie. Did I mention that Madison also has really long, blonde hair—perfect for tug-of-war? Then there's Alex. He's in first grade, and my favorite, primarily because I'm quickly going to be bigger and stronger than him, so he's the one I'm in charge of. That brings me to Mom. She's simply the best. She feeds and hangs with me every day, usually providing at least a couple of walks through the neighborhood. I also remember catching her eye during their visit when I was just a baby. I fully realize it's because of her that I'm lucky enough to live here now. She gave me that look of love. And as Humphrey Bogart once said, "I think this is the beginning of a beautiful friendship."

CHAPTER 2

THE DOG ATE MY HOMEWORK

From the ripe age of six months, Cooper had been proving his above-average intelligence. When he was around ten months old, he began his training as an escape artist and quickly adopted the nickname, Houdini. We would come home to a mangled crate alongside an ecstatic, excited, and extremely proud dog meeting us at the door. The normal metal crate latches were an insult to his intelligence, and soon we had to "up our game." We won many battles by getting clever with how we locked the crate. But it wasn't too long before Cooper eventually won the war and was left on his own to roam while we were gone during the day. The main damage to the house then was dog urine from Cooper marking his territory. I'm not going to even call it peeing, he was strictly making a point. There were two primary targets. First, he would pee in Alex's room on his bed frame and comforter, just making sure that everyone knew he was in charge. Second, and only when he was mad at me, he would pee on the dirty clothes hamper in our room. It only took a few deep carpet cleanings until he was soon banned from upstairs. Fool us once, well, twice, thrice....

I remember when Cooper first escaped from his metal crate during the night. I awoke to something falling over downstairs and a thundering, noisy banging. I immediately shook Steve to wake him up and told him someone had broken into the house. Fortunately, I paused a minute before calling 911 to send Steve down to investigate as I sat trembling on the bed with my phone in hand, ready to hit send. Meanwhile, I should note that Fitzroy was still sleeping soundly right next to us, "perfectly." That's when I heard Steve yell, "COOPER!" followed by the slam of the door. Cooper had managed to open the metal door locks from his crate and was now free with no eyes on him, so, obviously, he entered the kitchen. He managed to open the garbage drawer handle with his teeth and then pull the bag up and out of the garbage can to enjoy a second dinner of chicken. This was the first of many gourmet garbage meals.

Speaking of chicken, we lucked out in the child department, and neither Madison nor Alex have any allergies. Both children are quite healthy and can eat whatever they like. In the dog department, however, we were not so lucky. After frequent trips to the vet with red bacteria-infected ears and itchy skin, we had Cooper allergy tested. It ends up—the dog who eats everything is also allergic to everything, most severely to poultry products, dairy, and wheat. If you have ever tried to find a dog food without poultry products, it is not an easy task. So now we spend twice the price for a thirty-pound bag of Lamb and Sweet Potato food for him, but at least he eats well.

It seemed as if Cooper learned new tricks every single day. I don't like to brag. I'm only pointing this out because I'm not talking about the basic sit, stay, or roll-over; Cooper was much more sophisticated. One beautiful spring afternoon, we were standing in the kitchen, enjoying happy hour with friends, when we heard a deafening, frenzied scratching, only to have the door into the house from the garage suddenly burst open and loudly slam against the wall. A hundred-pound brown monster stormed into the house. No!

18

It wasn't an intruder; it was only Cooper letting himself in. Apparently, Cooper had been studying the concept of doors, and our French door handles made things quite straightforward. Simply walk up the two garage steps, jump on the door, and flick the door handle with his paws to enter. On a positive note, from that point forward, we never had to open the door to let Cooper inside; he came in when he was ready. We did, however, have to constantly clean and repaint the door to the garage.

About the same time, he'd mastered the art of letting himself in from outside, he learned that if he jumped against the front door when the main door was open, the glass storm door would magically allow him freedom. His favorite daily activity was to stare out the glass door until someone walked by, and then pounce outside, down the stairs, and run to the yard perimeter vehemently (but harmlessly) barking and scaring the unsuspecting passerby to death, all while excessively wagging his tail. His ultimate favorite person to terrorize was Deborah, our neighbor. Every day, Deborah would walk by with her two small pugs, each about the size of Cooper's head. He would go through his routine, Deborah would jump back and gasp, and I would follow him out, apologizing profusely. It was a daily routine we all got used to. We always assumed Deborah hated us and Cooper; but years later when we were moving, she pulled me aside and said how much she was going to miss Cooper. She viewed him as the neighborhood protector.

Aww, see, even Deborah couldn't help but love him.

It did take Cooper a while to learn the art of bag opening. As a puppy, he ruined countless school backpacks when one of the kids left their half-eaten lunch boxes in them. He also destroyed Madison's friend Katy's Vera Bradley duffle bag when she dared to enter for a sleepover with a late-night bag of candy hidden in her bag. You'll hear much more about this acquired skill later.

Our family also quickly learned that some of the legendary school excuses can actually be valid. We, specifically, could very much relate to the "my dog ate my homework excuse." In third grade, Alex had the dreaded "Cereal Box" book report. He had to read a book and then create a book report by decorating a cereal box with pictures and a summary of the book. Not to say that he waited until the last minute, BUT… the night before the project was due, Alex was finishing (or should I say, *I* was finishing) up the project. Finally, it was done, and the true art masterpiece was carefully placed on the kitchen counter so it wouldn't get crushed in his backpack. When we came downstairs the next morning, I almost tripped over the destroyed box on the stairs and the guilty looking dog lying next to it sadly looking down and away from me. I promptly and furiously took a picture of the torn-up project, printed it, and had Alex take the picture to school to see if Mrs. Pumo would possibly give him an extra day to complete his project. Let me just say, this project was not fun the first time, but was absolutely miserable the second time.

What really happened

BREAKING IN THE FAMILY

Journal entries from the winter of 2010/2011

I mentioned that the torture chamber would not be a long-term thing. It was horrendous to be stuck in that 3x5 jail cell while Fitzroy smugly would lie right in front of me, flaunting his freedom, playing with his toy—a stupid hedgehog. I soon learned the metal latches on my chamber could easily slide. With one quick flip-up with the nose, I was free to go.

Plenty of dogs can open doors to go outside, but I venture to guess that I'm one of the brilliant few who has mastered the art of home entry via doorknob. It did take quite a bit of trial and error but, what can I say, I'm persistent, and it paid off. I had to get inside to find the backpacks! Did I mention that I'm not even a year old yet?

Woohoo, I have allergies! I'm so excited. Most dogs have to eat boring chicken every single day of their lives. I can't even imagine something that dreadful and boring. I'm so lucky, Mom decided to splurge and get me lamb and sweet potato, the combination is exquisite.

I don't know what Mom is talking about when she says I "terrorize" Deborah. I just love visiting with other dogs, and when they walk by every day, I have to say hello. My theory is, why does she continue to walk by MY house on a daily basis if she didn't want to see ME. Mom should be thanking me for being the neighborhood protector. I've always known that Deborah secretly liked me. She looks at me the same way Mom did when we first met.

I am so sad and depressed. Recently, Fitzroy crossed over to that place they call the Rainbow Bridge. All I want to do is sleep. I think I also may have lost my appetite, no, wait, that's just silly, I have to eat. Actually, there's this thing called grief binge eating, maybe that's what's wrong with me? Fitzroy had finally come around and loved spending time with me. Once I had my freedom, we had cherished our cuddle time together on the steps, especially when no one else was around.

Now, about that stupid empty cardboard box. I truly am quite sorry, if I had known it was empty, I never would've opened it. Believe me, I was equally as disappointed as Mom was angry. I am not a fan of glue and paper.

I'm going to hold my comments on those mysteriously lumpy contraptions with many hidden compartments that they call backpacks and luggage until a later time. Something tells me I'll have lots more to say on the topic, so let's just chalk it up to "training" for the moment.

CHAPTER THREE

DOG PARK EXPULSION

It may seem like I'm only sharing the negative stories about Cooper, but he truly is a loving companion, despite all of the trouble he gets into. His favorite part of the day, other than eating, is walking with the kids to the bus stop. Every morning at precisely 8:07, Alex, Madison, Cooper, and I would walk out the door, down a few houses, and across the street to the bus stop. We would wait patiently for the school bus to arrive. The kids would hug him and then mysteriously disappear for a long eight hours.

Immediately after the bus stop was "walk/run time." Daily, I would take Cooper on a three to five-mile walk or run. I had never been a true runner but for some reason had always placed "running a marathon" on my bucket list. On the year of my fortieth birthday, I discovered that the Chicago Marathon was occurring on my actual birthday. It was now or never. I'm proud to say I have now checked that item off the bucket list. The experience was incredible, but the training was so time-consuming. I was always grateful to have a faithful running buddy by my side. No one is going to bother me with a hundred-pound brown bear look-alike by my side.

The only challenge with Cooper on runs/walks was the crazy excessive peeing on absolutely EVERYTHING! I understand that dogs mark their territory to communicate, but come on, this is ridiculous. I must have the most social dog on the planet. The kids and I once counted the number of "pee stops" on a short mile walk and lost count at 148. I remember thinking "Maybe he has a problem, maybe I should ask Google," but soon forgot and went on with my day.

When Fitzroy was younger, I had always taken him a few blocks down to a park to run around with the neighborhood dogs. We would stay for about thirty minutes, and Fitz would run and play and fetch with all of his friends. Logically, I thought the dog park would be a fantastic way to wear out Cooper and couldn't wait for him to get old enough to socialize. At about one year of age, I figured he was finally old enough to join in on the fun. Once we arrived, he immediately bounded into the park, creating chaos with the other park-goers by stealing balls, frisbees, knocking into people, and humping the other dogs. I was horrified. The "dog people," as I call them, didn't know what hit them. They began whispering and pointing, all while maintaining a safe distance. I returned a few times, figuring I could "break them in" and things would get better. I do, however, like to pride myself on being perceptive, and quickly observed that as we approached the park, most of the patrons would cringe and begin rounding up their dogs. A few folks came around. Dave was great, he had a yellow lab named Chase and lived adjacent to the park. He had a lab, so of course, he understood. Chase and Cooper hit it off and routinely stole each other's toys and treats with zero issues. Then there was an older man, I will call Bob, with his small, yappy, white schnauzer, Penny.

One morning, on a day that I'm certain is still talked about by the dog people, Cooper was somewhat behaving himself.

I was thinking to myself, I'm so glad I stuck this out, I knew they would come around. I might actually even make a few friends here. Then it happened. Cooper returned from fetching a ball and suddenly ran over to Penny and peed on her. YES, that's right—I said he peed on his friend! Who lifts their leg on their friends? Let me just say that Bob did not appreciate this behavior in the least. We were immediately banned from the dog park, and I was mortified. People were even giving Bob their extra baggies to try and wipe poor little Penny off. I didn't realize you could get banned from the dog park! From then on, if I saw Bob and Penny out during a walk, I would always immediately turn the corner in shame. I guess it was time to find a new running route.

What really happened

LESSON LEARNED: DON'T PEE ON YOUR FRIENDS

Journal entries from the fall of 2010

Mom is right, my favorite part of the day is walking the kids to the bus stop. Well, it's my favorite time other than meals. It also means that my walk or run is next. I love the days when it includes the long run. Running is so relaxing, and my afternoon naps on those days are the best. I do have a question though. Madison and Alex disappear every day in a long yellow box for eight dreadfully long hours, where could they possibly be going, why are they leaving me, and why isn't mom panicking?

I have to address the so-called "excessive peeing." Of course, Mom always tells people that I sometimes pee a little on Alex's bed or the dirty clothes, but it really is an endearing gesture. I miss my family, and anyone who knows anything about dogs knows that this is a completely normal natural instinct, and it shows you that we were there.

As for the outside marking, research shows that when I "mark my territory" I am simply asserting my social status, looking for potential mates, and getting information on any unfamiliar dogs in the area. I also read somewhere on a place called Google (human words are weird) that a dog bladder allows for the release of just a little at a time, repeatedly and often. You people have social media and need to realize that being single is incredibly challenging for us dogs of today who can never be off-leash or outside alone. How am I supposed to meet anyone? The bottom line, Mom just needs to lighten up on my marking habit. She, out of everyone in my family, needs to remember that whenever she sees someone she knows outside on a walk, she talks and talks and talks FOREVER—I am simply expressing "my voice" and am not doing anything wrong or anything she doesn't do.

Lastly, I need to defend myself regarding the whole "Penny thing." If I'm being honest, I have to say… I just don't like the dog, and this was not an endearing gesture. I'm sure you've all had "that" kid in school who taunted you endlessly and sooner or later you just snap, doing something you regret. What can I say? I snapped. But I am truly am sorry (not sorry) if that counts for anything. Penny is so bossy and always thinks she is in charge. She weighs a whole fifteen pounds; how could *she* be in charge? Mom needs to remember that I am technically a puppy, and my brain is still developing. At the end of the day, it was ME who suffered the consequences and now can't play with Chase and my other friends, all because of that annoying Penny.

CHAPTER FOUR

WELCOME TO PURE MICHIGAN

I'm not saying that Cooper didn't love his home in Park Ridge, but a tiny quarter-acre lot doesn't give much room for fun dog activities such as swimming, fetching the ball, and stealing shoes. And did I mention an endless flow of guests to play with? Much like us, from the very first time Cooper arrived at our Michigan lake home in Grand Haven, he was in love. The home sits on top of a hill overlooking the lake with a large one and a quarter acre lot of green grass in between. What's not to love? Every summer weekend, we would pile in the car early on Thursday afternoons to make the drive. We had to strategically plan our departure time to avoid the Chicago weekend traffic, which can quickly turn a three-hour drive into five-plus hours.

I still remember the first time Cooper made the journey. Once we got about an hour out of Chicago, we stopped at a drive through. Per the usual routine, Madison had brought her good friend, Allison, along for the weekend. We stopped at McDonald's, and everyone placed their order, except for Cooper of course. I passed out the food to everyone as Cooper quietly stalked like a lion, ready to pounce on his unsuspecting prey. Allison unwrapped her cheeseburger, and faster than she could bring the burger from the wrapper to her mouth—GULP—Cooper grabbed the burger, and it magically disappeared without even a bite. The only remnant of the crime was a satisfied tongue sweep across the mouth just in case there were any bun or ketchup crumbs on his nose. Needless to say, I currently need two hands to count the number of unsuspecting kids and adults who have since fallen victim to this crime on the car ride to Michigan.

One thing I'm known for in Michigan is my Cooper Rules. Upon the arrival of any guest, before they take suitcases to their rooms, everyone is victim to my welcome speech. First and foremost, I ask that any food in their luggage be brought to the kitchen, or their bags will be opened and searched by our 104-pound scavenger. I then issue a warning that while visiting, if you ever leave any food unattended, it will be stolen. This includes everything from your plate at the dinner table to a stray marshmallow waiting to be toasted.

I met a new friend, Lindsi, while Alex was at the University of Michigan swim camp—Yes, you heard that correctly, Mom met a friend at camp. Even though Madison was horrified. "Mom's aren't supposed to meet friends at a kids camp!" Alex was too young to stay in the dorms, so I had booked a local hotel for the week to hang in Ann Arbor. I would drop him off early in the morning for camp, and then have the day to myself, working, jogging around campus, and exploring the beautiful town of Ann Arbor. On the first day, as the campers left to follow their respective coaches, I noticed that Alex and two other boys were aimlessly wandering in the direction of the older kids and not having a clue where to go. In the stands, I shook my head and laughed to myself when I saw another woman doing the same. Now, more than eight years later, Lindsi and her

31

family have become such wonderful, dear friends. The moms and boys alike love spending time together. We've never lived anywhere near each other, but it never fails that one of us will call the other to say we'll be in town, and we always manage to meet up for an adventure. I put Lindsi on my shortlist of people you are destined to meet in your lifetime. Marybeth, who gave me the idea of Cooper, is on that list too.

Two weeks after camp, I invited Lindsi and her boys to spend the night as they traveled through upper Michigan. Upon arrival, I gave my "food in suitcase" speech, to which she replied, "no food, only wine" and proceeded to her room. We soon left for the afternoon to enjoy the sun, lunch, drinks, and some musical entertainment at the Bil-Mar, our local beach restaurant, so the kids could play in the sand while we chatted. The boys occupied themselves by building sand balls for two+ hours on the beach, only stopping for a necessary ice cream sundae break. We got home a few hours later. As I was building a fire outside in the fire pit, Lindsi came out of her room, laughing, to let me know that apparently there had been some food in her suitcase. Her mother had put a box of Weetabix cereal in her bag. Cooper carefully, but strategically, unzipped the suitcase and took out only the cereal for an early dinner. If you've ever seen Weetabix, it is like thin strands of wheat pressed together. To this day, we likely still have remnants of the Weetabix smashed into our carpet.

What really happened

I THINK I'M GONNA LIKE IT HERE

Journal entries from 2010 & 2011

Now we're talking—*this* is a house. So many places to run around, and the water—this place is the absolute BEST. It's going to take me a while to master my surroundings, but I think I'm going to like it here.

The drive up wasn't so bad either, they drove through this fascinating place that just hands you food through a magic window, how awesome is that! BUT they clearly forgot someone—ME! I can't even take credit for this one, stealing that burger from Allison was easier than taking candy away from a baby (not that I've ever done that, but to be fair, I haven't been around many babies). It was inches from my nose, and everyone knows how sensitive a dog's nose is. She shouldn't complain, they turned around and went through another magic window, so she still got her food. See, everyone wins! I don't know why Mom was so upset with me.

As always, Mom failed to give me credit for not ruining Lindsi's suitcase. I very carefully unzipped her bag, but I just knew there was something inside. Did I mention I was bored? They had rudely left me at dinner time and didn't feed me before they left; leaving me to fend for myself. They never tell me how long they're going to be gone, so I have to make sure I don't starve. I honestly have to say that I was a bit sorry after demolishing the Weetabix because it made me SOOO thirsty; I've had cardboard tastier than that awful cereal! I had already finished my bowl of water, and no one left a toilet lid open. Although I have now mastered opening suitcases, I did not yet know how to lift the toilet lid, and that isn't a priority of mine.

Another benefit of this lake house is that there is a constant supply of unsuspecting visitors. These people typically arrive with multiple small children who are outstanding. Mom continues to give her "little speech" whenever people come, but what she doesn't realize is that no one listens. People are so ready to go enjoy the lake and surrounding activities that keeping a close eye on their food is the absolute last thing on their minds. Not to worry, I'm always listening, and I'm guessing this will not be the last time you hear about me helping myself to meals.

CHAPTER FIVE

LIFE IS BETTER ON A BOAT

Not only does Michigan have a sprawling yard the size of a park, but there is also WATER and a BOAT—better known as heaven to all of us and Cooper. The twenty-four-foot open bow Four Winn Boat has a large wrap-around seat in front to allow for maximum wind. Cooper loves nothing more than to join us for a trip up the river to get gas. He has never learned to understand or accept why he doesn't get invited on the tubing, skiing, or most of the boat rides, and why most of the time he gets left up at the house. Don't worry, you'll soon learn more.

If I am famous for my "welcome speeches" that few acknowledge or pay attention to, Steve is known for his "boat rules." He typically waits until several kids come sprinting full speed down the long dock to yell, "No running on the dock!" I think maybe once there was a friend of Alex's who slowed down to a slow jog, but usually he's wasting his breath. Another equally broken rule is his "drip dry rule." After a tubing or skiing run, as people climb up the ladder onto the back ledge of the boat, ninety percent of the time, the kids immediately hop into the boat as water streams endlessly off of them, forming a puddle on the carpeted floor of the boat. About that time, Steve typically yells "Drip Dry!" I'm still not quite sure what this accomplishes, but it makes him feel better.

One hot summer day, the first-year Cooper was in Michigan, we were all enjoying life, hanging on our dock, when I had a GREAT IDEA. Let me start by saying "enjoying life" in this instance means that the adults were indulging in a couple of my infamous afternoon "Blue Drinks" that I make in my Margaritaville Machine. I religiously enjoy mine in my Cubs Tervis Tumbler with friends and/or family on the dock. I share the blue drinks. I do NOT share my Cubs Tervis Tumbler. We started discussing how it would be a good idea to take Cooper tubing with the kids. "After all, he probably loves it even more than they do, and NEVER gets to go," I pleaded. From the get-go, Steve thought my great idea was absolutely awful. "What could go wrong?" was my reply. After some taunting from myself, our friends the Scullys, and four pre-teens ages seven to thirteen, we convinced Steve to let us take him. We decided that Steve would drive; our friend, Tim, would follow on the wave-runner; the kids would hold him on the tube; I would be the spotter on the boat; and our trusty friend, Diane, would capture memories of the experience. We all pulled away from the dock, and for the first time ever, we allowed Cooper to join us for a tubing run. A few minutes later, when we were out on the open lake, the kids jumped on the tube. Cooper instantly followed. So far, so good! Steve started driving. At first, Cooper was enjoying the ride! He was sandwiched between Madison and Alex, each with a firm grip on his collar. Soon, he realized how close he was to the water, and decided it might be more fun to jump in for a swim. Let me backtrack for a minute and say, everyone who tubes has to wear a life jacket. Well, that includes Cooper. Back at the dock, we had found a jacket that was the perfect fit. We put his front paws through the armholes and buckled it around his belly. How cute did he look, and what an awesome photo opportunity! The problem was, Cooper was so used to swimming without a life jacket that he was freaked out and couldn't figure out how to swim with it on. We hadn't thought of that. He was frantically paddling in circles, unsure of where to go or how to get there. We were all calling his name, and the kids jumped in after him. I jumped in next to the boat ladder, and we were finally able to coax him to me. We pulled him up the ladder, only for him to promptly shake on Steve. Not even Cooper follows the drip-dry rule! Gotta love wet dog water. To date, that was Cooper's one and only tubing experience, but stay tuned for many more water adventures to follow. Since that point, Cooper has been restricted to the leisurely sunset cruises where he can sit in the front of the boat and act like Leonardo DiCaprio— "I'm King of the World!"

After the failed tubing experience, we started leaving Cooper inside in his crate during our tubing/skiing runs. This did not go over well in Cooper's mind. He went from being free on the dock and boat to being inside by himself locked up. Initially, it was a great idea but, as at home, it didn't last long once he figured out how to escape from the "unescapable" crate that Google advertised in marketing materials. It was becoming a game of which was the lesser of two evils for us. He would either escape from his crate and then roam the house stealing food, OR be left solo on the dock where he would promptly steal shoes from those he was angry at, typically Steve or myself.

What really happened

TUBING IS OVER-RATED!

Journal entries from summer 2011

I used to think car rides were fun, but the boat is incredible— I'm on top of the world, and there is an endless supply of wind that I can stick my nose into as we drive. Mom always nabs the best spot up front, but I usually manage to take it from her, or at least sit on her lap, which she loves. I don't get to go very often, but I do usually get the invite for a leisurely sunset cruise, and sometimes the cruise upriver for gas.

She's got the tubing thing all wrong. I never wanted to get on the tube, I only wanted to get on the boat. I was trying to save the kids on the tube which is the only reason I hopped on. Come on, no way did I want to get on the tube in the embarrassing life jacket. How am I supposed to swim in this contraption? Of course, they had to document the moment with an endless supply of photos for Facebook.

I have learned most of my mastery Houdini skills from the dungeon in Michigan. They frequently have the nerve to go out on the boat and lock me up in the dungeon—NOT FAIR, especially after giving me a taste of the excitement I was missing. I started playing around with the locks and soon realized they were easy to open. When they started getting creative, I had to up my game and get creative too. They won a few of the battles when I couldn't get out, but soon they gave up and stopped putting me in there. In my opinion, they may have won some battles, but I won the war.

CHAPTER SIX

DOG DAYS (& NIGHTS) OF SUMMER

Another one of the great things about summertime in Michigan is the meal routines. As with most things, some rules apply. My rule for Michigan dinner has always been that if it can't be prepared on the grill, it doesn't get prepared. No oven allowed.

I am typically an early morning riser, meaning 7:30/8:00 am in Michigan; so, nothing crazy. Once up, I frequently head to the local vegetable market for fresh Michigan produce and the grocery store to pick up items for dinner that evening. I immediately prep all of the food so we don't have to worry about it later in the day. This entails cutting the vegetables and wrapping them in foil. We can then forget about it and spend the day on the lake.

One special treat at Green Acres, the local fruit and vegetable market, is their locally made fresh and delicious blueberry bread. In the early years, I would frequently stop on the way into town but made the mistake of doing this once with Cooper in the car. On the less than five-minute drive to our home from Green Acres, Cooper managed to secretly and silently devour two entire loaves. After this experience, I stopped going on our way into town and have made it part of my morning weekend routine. One weekend, we had our friends, the Abdalas up for the weekend and were enjoying some coffee and fresh blueberry bread for breakfast on our upstairs deck. As we were reminiscing about the evening before, Erica was midsentence when suddenly a large brown blob swooped in and grabbed her entire piece of bread right in front of all of us. It is not surprising he managed to steal some food. What was a bit shocking was how bold he had become to do it right in front of me and Steve. That usually NEVER happened.

When dinner time arrives, a few of us usually begin grilling, guests and the kids play Ladder ball and Bags, while Steve begins assembling the fire pit. The mere fact that guests and kids are playing the yard games presents an immediate opportunity for Cooper. When the kids were younger, it never failed—a few minutes into the game, I would hear "MOM, Cooper stole the ____ (fill in the blank)." I routinely ignored this statement or told them to get it from him, I'm busy. This then resulted in a thirty-minute game of keep away. Cooper would take the item, confidently jaunt down the hill, lie down, and drop the item in front of him. The kids then would run down the hill and try to grab it. When they got about five feet away, Cooper would grab it and run away to his new location. This game typically continues until Steve or I get involved, and Cooper realizes fun is over. He would then retreat and usually get locked inside for a while (until someone runs out and leaves the door open).

The grill master also needs to be on constant watch. We have a large outdoor table where we place the food waiting to be grilled in the foil packets. Another one of Cooper's favorite activities is to grab an ear of corn or a veggie foil packet and run down the hill with it. We frequently find him lying on the lawn enjoying his corn, cob and all.

Once dinner is served, the routine is to place all the food on the basement bar, buffet style, and have people go through and help themselves. It never fails. Cooper strategically places himself off to the side, quietly assessing his prey. With full plates, the adults proceed outside to the patio table, while the kids head upstairs to the deck. Cooper wisely follows the kids upstairs, knowing there will be at least one unsuspecting child not paying attention. He's patient, and the split-second a plate of food is left unguarded, he attacks. Soon we have a child running downstairs crying "Cooper ate my hamburger." There is only one thing that is guaranteed: if we're paying attention ninety percent of the time, Cooper is paying attention a hundred of the time. He rarely comes up empty-handed. Over the years, we have learned to always make at least two extra of whatever is on the menu.

After dinner is s'mores time. We all surround the fire pit and, once the fire is "ready," it's time to break out the s'mores. I had to mention the fire being ready because this is and always has been a very important detail for Steve, a former Eagle Scout, otherwise known to us as the Fire Master. It is absolutely NOT allowed to cook s'mores too early, despite frequent pleading from the "starving children in Michigan." Once we get the all-clear from Steve that the fire is ready, the kids bring out the marshmallows, graham crackers, chocolate, and the roasting sticks. This is a perfect setting for

Cooper. Picture this—a dark patio where it's especially hard to see brown-lurking scavengers. Add to that, everyone is concerned with roasting their own "perfect" marshmallow or assembling their s'more. Quite frequently, not one person would be paying attention to the remaining marshmallows, chocolate, and graham crackers lying on the table. I can't count the number of times Cooper has scored big during this activity.

Any lake day is not complete without the end of day clean-up. Once it gets late and everyone retreats to bed after a long day of sun, fun, and lake libations, it can be easy to forget to empty the trash and clean-up any left-over food. Although Cooper sleeps in our bedroom with the door shut, early in the morning he gains full house access while we typically lounge in bed a bit longer than he does. Another of his guaranteed maneuvers is for Cooper to "make his rounds" throughout the house, scouring every countertop, coffee table, and garbage can for anything remaining. I would guestimate his success rate is approximately seventy-five percent—he typically finds something. His biggest score yet was the remaining half of Tina Paxhia's birthday cake. To this day, she has still not forgiven him for that. Even if he fails inside, he will proceed outside to the large garbage can. Should it be even slightly full, he jumps up and nudges the lid open with his nose, pulls the full garbage bag out, and tears it apart all over the driveway. We have labeled this the "jump and grab," and Cooper excels at it.

By the way, Cooper's skill at opening the French door handles also works in our Michigan house.

What really happened

I'M SMARTER THAN YOUR 5TH GRADER

Journal entries summer 2011 – present day

Who doesn't love fresh Michigan blueberries in the summertime? It's Mom's fault for stopping at Green Acres with me in the car for the highly requested blueberry bread and vegetables. The car was full, so the box was placed in the back of the car right next to me. I'd always heard everyone raving about how good the blueberry bread is. I HAD to try it, but I didn't touch the vegetables! They were correct, it was amazing; so, of course, I had to finish the loaf. It's their fault for having the music on too loud. They didn't even hear me. After that experience, they never let me go with to Green Acres again. But finally, I got to taste the delectable melt in your mouth bread! Last summer our friends, the Abdalas were up for the weekend. Mom and Dad were sitting with them chatting and laughing about the silly things they had done the night before. Erica wasn't exactly paying attention, and I just couldn't help myself, it was so close and smelled so good—what can I say, she was an easy target, and easy targets are my favorite people. Why does it take humans so long to eat food? It was fair game. That will teach them for grounding me from Green Acres.

Not all of my entertainment is centered around food; I love it when Alex and his friends play Ladder Ball and Bags. It is so much fun to steal their stuff. When Mom and Dad play, I get in trouble. But with the kids, it always takes at least fifteen minutes before they involve Mom and Dad. During that time, they chase me around the yard—it's fantastic, and they NEVER learn! I also don't understand why people always say, "you can't teach an old dog new tricks," because in my experience, the saying should be "you can't teach young children anything." They never learn that I am faster and wiser than all of them. I'll run down the hill a safe distance from everyone and pick my spot. Then I tauntingly drop the sought-after item, for example, a ball. This move always results in a stream of kids running down toward me, screaming. They actually think that they're going to get to me and take the ball before I'm smart enough to pick it up and change locations!

Mom really makes me mad when she tells stories about me stealing the kids' dinners. They make a big deal about setting up the food on the basement bar and letting everyone "help themselves." Does she think I don't listen when she says, "dinner is ready, come make your plate"? After all, I am always the first one to arrive and to be waiting for my turn. Then she says, "Kids, go upstairs to eat on the patio table." That is exactly what I do. I follow them up. I don't have two hands to make my plate, so I patiently wait until one of the kids runs away from the table for something—which always happens. Then I quickly help myself. After all, they were done. I also remember once hearing Mom talking about one of the best benefits of having a dog is that you don't need a vacuum, because they clean it up for you. I am just trying to do my part and clean up a little bit—she should be thanking me.

As for the s'mores—come on. Freshly cooked roasted marshmallows, who can resist?

CHAPTER SEVEN

WATER BED

It didn't take Cooper long to become obsessed with joining us on frequent weekend getaways to the lake. One day, we were packing the car for an afternoon at the beach in Michigan. I had the window open so the car didn't get too hot as we were preparing to go. We all were very deliberately keeping the doors shut, and would only strategically open them to prevent Cooper from jumping in the car and trying to "hide" so he could join us. However, we had a passenger window open. I went inside to grab some extra towels. When I returned, the kids were laughing hysterically. Cooper was sitting in the driver's side seat, very, very proud of himself. I quickly blamed the kids for opening the door and letting him in, but it turns out that Cooper jumped through the window! I'm still not quite sure how he did it, because he was larger than the opening, but the hair and drool surrounding the door made it apparent that is what happened. I only wish I would've witnessed the actual act, or better yet, caught it on video. I promptly opened the car door, pulled the stubborn beast out of the car and into the house, and we drove away to the beach.

The weather could not have been more perfect: crystal-blue sky and water, eighty-degree temperatures, and no clouds in sight. We spent a glorious afternoon at the beach and were gone for about five hours. That evening, we came home and sat outside by the fire pit to finish the night off with perfectly cooked s'mores. One of the many great things about Michigan is that during the summer, the sun does not set until close to ten p.m. around 10:30/11:00, I was exhausted and headed up to sleep. I threw on my pajamas and hopped into bed. All of a sudden, the kids heard the most blood-curdling scream of all time coming from my room. "C-O-O-P-E-R!!!!"

Cooper had not only spent the afternoon lounging on my bed, but he had peed exactly where I sleep to demonstrate how upset he had been at me for taking him out of the car and leaving him alone earlier in the day. He tried to sulk off with the look of a child who had just had his hand caught in the cookie jar, but I grabbed his collar and pulled him outside. I ranted at the kids that they were not to let him inside, and for them to let him sleep outside for the night. I tossed the sheets in the washing machine and rummaged through the cleaning supplies to find something to clean the mattress with. But not before calling and yelling at Steve, who of course could do absolutely nothing from Chicago. I'm sure he was thankful he wasn't with me in Michigan.

After a while, the kids were upset that something would happen to Cooper if we left him outside all night, but I refused to give in. Two hours later, as I finished the cleaning and slammed my door to finally go to bed, I was aware that they had already opened the front door and snuck Cooper into their room. I pretended not to know, as I tearfully Googled places to send your dog for specialized training or places that take dogs who can't behave. I was exhausted but could not sleep, I could only seethe with anger in my bed. How could my intuition have been so wrong in selecting Cooper out of all the other puppies? I'm normally very perceptive.

What really happened

SWEET REVENGE

Journal entry, July 2014

It was a beautiful day, the car was loaded with beach toys, and I love the beach. I thought, "there is absolutely no way they are going to the beach while I stay home by myself." The doors to the car were all shut, so I had no other choice but to jump in the window. I knew it was going to be a tight squeeze, but I thought if I aimed correctly and had the right amount of thrust, I could do it. Ready, set, go—YES, I made it!! I remember thinking, sun, fun, and beach, here I come! Let's get this show on the road. Wait a minute. Why were the kids laughing so hard? More importantly, why was Mom yelling like someone just stole her bone? No way, I could not believe she actually opened the door and pulled me out of the very car I just worked so hard to get into. Then she dragged me inside. I tried to put my leg locks on, but that didn't stop her. She still dragged me. They couldn't leave me, they couldn't leave me! Oh no, they just left me as I looked out the window and saw the car driving away.

I couldn't believe the amount of sadness that overcame me. Now I was left all alone with no one to hang out with. I missed Mom so much, and what if they never came back home? Maybe I'd feel better if I went to sleep in her room for a while. Let me share that Mom and Dad didn't let me sleep in their bed, they said I was too big, but there was plenty of room for us all in their nice queen size bed. Let me

52

just jump up here and lay down on Mom's pillow so I can smell her. Maybe that will help. One hour alone. Let me go get a drink out of the toilet, which by the way, is much better than the water in my bowl. It's so cold and fresh. Back up on the bed; two hours alone. Okay, now I was getting worried. What if they didn't come back? I could starve to death. I better go find a snack. Yes! The kids left some popcorn on the basement coffee table, perfect for an afternoon snack. Back up on the bed; three hours alone. Are you kidding me? They still weren't home? Now I was getting worried, I hoped they were okay; they have NEVER been gone this long. I better go get another snack. Back up on the bed; four hours alone. Now I was just mad; it was ridiculous they left me like this. I tried to fall asleep to make the time go faster. Oh no, I shouldn't have had all of that water! Now I had wet the bed. They couldn't be mad at me, it was an accident. Wait, was that the garage door? Everything was better; now they were home. The kids burst through the door and gave me hugs, and then we ran downstairs for s'more time, YAY! I'll get some nighttime snacks now. Life was good.

I couldn't figure out why Mom was so mad when she yelled and pulled me outside. Earlier in the day, she pulled me *inside*. Could she please make up her mind? Wait, she must've found the accident on her bed. I really didn't mean to. I'm sorry! Normally when I give a simple bark, they'd immediately open the door, but this time there was no response, so I started to scratch. I didn't understand why they weren't listening to me. It was dark out there with scary raccoons and possums. They had better open this door quickly before I got attacked! Pretty soon, Madison quietly opened the door and snuck me into her room. I couldn't understand why; I've never slept there. I always slept in Mom's room, but oh well, Madison and Allison were curled up on the floor with me, giving me tons of attention, so this was pretty fantastic.

CHAPTER EIGHT

WOODWORKING

Once Cooper started escaping from his crate, it became evident that we had to do something to protect our recently remodeled kitchen cabinets—at this rate, he was stealing food daily, ruining at least one cabinet door per week. Cooper would enter the kitchen and first quickly stake out the cabinets containing food and/or garbage. Next, he would scratch or use his mouth to open the cabinet and simply help himself. Our kitchen had been remodeled three short years earlier with beautiful dark cherry custom cabinets, many of which now contained quarter-inch deep nail scratches all over them. Mind you, the cabinets containing plates, glasses, and silverware were miraculously untouched.

For years, we have had an outdoor Invisible Fence, which we purchased for Fitzroy because we did not have a yard that could easily be fenced in. The Invisible Fence is a buried underground wire installed around the perimeter of the yard. A dog then wears a collar that is part of the invisible fence package. When the dog ventures near the perimeter, they hear a high-pitched "beep, beep, beep." If they keep going and cross the line, they receive a light shock. Our dogs have very little in common, but they both were petrified of receiving the shock and never crossed the fence. Fitzroy loved nothing more than to leisurely lay in the front yard all day long on a nice sunny day. He never barked and rarely even stood to greet the occasional passerby. Fitz was also known to receive several treats from strangers on a daily basis who merely enjoyed stopping by to pet him during their

daily stroll. As I mentioned before, everyone loved him—
"the perfect dog."

One day, our Invisible Fence line was mistakenly cut by the
landscaper during yard work. What started as a nuisance to
deal with ended up being one of the best things that ever
happened. The Invisible Fence repairman came out to make
the repair. When I started talking to him about how we liked
their system and how long we had been using their product,
I made one of my typical sarcastic comments: "I just wish
you had something like this I could use inside for my
kitchen." My prayers were answered. THEY HAD AN
INDOOR UNIT!

It was a quite simple concept, a round disc-shaped unit
resembling a smoke detector that you placed in the vicinity
of where you wanted to keep the dog away from. You
plugged the unit in and played around with the distance
gauge until you got the desired distance. If the dog entered
that area, they received the same beeps and shock as they
would outside.

I'll never forget one Sunday afternoon around 5:00 pm. I was
coming home from producing the elementary school variety
show all weekend. It was a long, eighty+ hours at Roosevelt
School over the weekend with 400+ kids and their parents.
Let's just say, I was physically and emotionally exhausted. I
had long since lost any of the sense of humor I had two days
earlier. As we walked through the door, Cooper met us, but
immediately ran outside without even stopping to say hello.

We walked through the door. The whole main floor looked like a tornado had furiously swept through. The Lazy Susan cabinet where we kept all of the kid's snacks was EMPTY. Four cereal boxes, twenty-four personal size bags of chips, a box of Kraft Macaroni & Cheese, and a destroyed Oreo cookie bag—GONE! Cooper had hosted a large party while we were away.

Steve was traveling, so it was up to the kids and me to clean up the mess. The worst was the wet, slimy macaroni and cheese powder that was now giving my cream-colored stairway landing carpet an orange glow. I couldn't figure out how he had gotten into the kitchen, as we had his collar on him. Later I realized the battery had run out, and Cooper's determination had won this battle. Since then, we've learned that whenever Cooper meets us at the door, avoids eye contact, and runs outside without a hello kiss, that he has been up to something. At that point, I was so distraught that I called Steve that evening to discuss the real possibility of sending him away for extensive training or, worst case, having to give him up. He was so naughty, and I really couldn't take much more. I whole-heartedly believe in my heart that dogs are true family members. I don't think I could ever actually do that, but Cooper was testing me to the fullest.

As a result of his naughtiness, a few years later, when we decided to sell our house, we needed to replace five kitchen cabinet doors that he'd ruined by opening them on a routine basis.

What really happened

ALL FOOD MUST GO TO THE "LAB" FOR TESTING

Journal entry, February 2011

Let's talk about the evil monster that now lives in my kitchen and likes to terrify me. Everyone has kryptonite, and for me, it's that scary circle monster. Sometimes it even moves on its own and falls over, scaring me even more. I can bravely open my metal crate and the kitchen cabinets, but if this darn monster is around me, I have to run and cower in the corner. I know I'm getting close if I get a deafening beep, beep, beep. After some training, I've gotten pretty good at knowing my boundaries.

Every once in a while, I think they decide to be nice and let me in. When I creep up to my normal stopping point, I don't hear a thing. Okay, a few steps closer, a few more. Wait, does this mean, I can help myself to a snack? I really didn't mean to clear out the entire cabinet, but it was so delicious. Now they're going to be mad because I forgot to clean-up after myself. I better immediately run out when they get home so they don't know it was me. They'll forget about it by the time I come inside. Just in case they don't, I'll give them the sad eye look that they just can't refuse. Mom hasn't been falling for that routine much lately, though. It might be time to come up with something else.

CHAPTER NINE

SAVING STEVE, SAVES COOPER

It was a typical school day morning, November 2, 2012, a day I will never forget. Two days after Halloween, the kids were eating breakfast. Steve had gone on a short three-mile run with Cooper before work. I was in my pajamas making lunches and a delicious breakfast smoothie (grapefruit, bananas, and clementine) in my recently purchased Vitamix blender with a magnificent Google rating, when the doorbell rang. First, let me revise the old saying my parents always told me as a teenager that "nothing good happens after midnight," by adding the phrase that "nothing good happens when your doorbell rings at 7:37 am on a Friday morning." I went to the door, with the kids peeking out behind me, and saw a stranger with Cooper. He then asked if I could please step outside. On second glance, I recognized the man as the very nice gentleman who frequently walked by our house on his morning walk with his dog and always said "hi" to our dogs. I had no idea what his name was, but wait again—WHY did he have Cooper, and WHERE was Steve? My heart was beating out of my chest. Did he get hit by a car? "Your husband passed out running," he said, "the ambulance just arrived, and they are a few blocks down the street."

Steve had passed out while running. Instead of running off, Cooper had calmly laid down next to Steve and began licking his face. As the nice man approached, he'd recognized Cooper. He and another good samaritan called 911 for help. He then walked Cooper back to our house to let me know. If it wasn't for the nice man recognizing Cooper while he stayed by Steve's side, he would never have known where to find me. Was he alive? Was he hurt? A million other questions and fears flooded my brain. "Do you want me to take the kids to the bus stop?" he asked. Suddenly I flashed back to reality and the fact the kids were on the other side of the door wondering what was happening and waiting for me to take them to the bus. "Kids, I've got to go get Dad, can you please go to the bus stop with this man?" YES, I sent my kids to the bus stop with a stranger. The lesson I had worked so hard to ingrain in their young brains was now thrown out the window.

I grabbed my keys and pulled eighty mph out of the driveway down the street to find Steve. It was literally only two blocks away, and I saw the red flashing lights. I parked in the middle of the street and ran over to Steve. I was still in my pink flannel pajamas that said "Life is Good" all over them and was wearing no shoes.

Steve had just regained consciousness, and the paramedics stopped me saying, "Ma'am your husband passed out but is now conscious. We're evaluating him. What hospital would you like us to take him to?"

What? They expected me to decide? Resurrection Hospital was less than a mile away and one of my closest friends, Beth, worked there as a nurse anesthetist. I knew I could get the inside scoop from her, as well as the VIP treatment. "Resurrection," I shouted out. "What happened? Is he okay?"

The paramedic interrupted me. I'll never forget his words, "Ma'am right now I'm more worried about you."

I said, "Really, I'm fine." Then I took a step back and realized I was in the middle of the street, barefoot, in my pajamas, basically hyperventilating. Whatever I did, I could not catch my breath, and my hands would not stop shaking.

"Take a breath, go home, change your clothes, and meet us at the hospital, your husband is stable," the paramedic said.

I immediately called Beth and told her Steve was on his way to the hospital and explained what had happened. She got right to work and contacted the ER doctor and cardiologist to let them know he needed VIP attention. WAIT A MINUTE—I just sent my kids to the bus stop with a stranger! I called my other friend, Jen, who always knows everything, and surprisingly she hadn't yet heard what happened. I asked her to go to school and make sure my kids were okay. "Tell them I talked to Steve and he's fine, they just need to send him to the hospital to get checked out and I'll update them later," I said.

I sped up to the hospital and arrived right behind the ambulance. They wheeled Steve into the ER, and I followed, still hyperventilating.

Over the next couple of days, they did a myriad of tests, and it turned out Steve had a mitral valve defect. It was something he had inherited since birth and had likely gotten worse over time. We found this odd because Steve had attended West Point and had extremely thorough physicals. Never before had anyone mentioned he even had a heart murmur. He was going to need open-heart surgery to try and repair or, worst case, possibly replace the valve. After a few scary months, thankfully, everything worked out well, and Steve completely recovered with his repaired mitral valve. He even started running again that next spring.

For the next few weeks, I would always pay attention in the mornings, looking for the "nice man" who saved Steve. I finally saw him one morning and ran outside to greet him with a hug. His name is Pat, and we had such a wonderful conversation. Pat had been so worried about what happened, but his dog had recently gotten ill, so he was no longer walking by our house daily. I got his address, and we sent a thank you gift and photo of Cooper and Steve to him. I haven't seen him in a while, but I still think about him frequently. We wish he and his family all the best.

I can't believe Cooper saved Steve! I was now feeling extremely guilty for my Google searches the past couple of months and for threatening to get rid of him. Phew, my judgment wasn't so wrong after all. Fitzroy would have definitely gone on a solo adventure if he had been with Steve when this happened. Cooper really is so sweet, if he could only control himself around food, he would be pretty perfect himself. Saving Steve, saved Cooper—from all my bad thoughts.

WHO'S PERFECT NOW

Journal entry, November 2012

It was the strangest thing, we were coming up on the end of our morning run and all of a sudden, Dad just fell into the grass to the right of the sidewalk and wasn't moving. It wasn't like Dad to play a joke like that with me. What was going on? Just like everyone else, I was terrified. He couldn't leave me! I must wake him up. I laid down next to him and began licking his face like I do every morning when it's time to wake up. He wasn't waking up. What was happening? I was so relieved when I saw my friend that passed by and petted me every morning. He knew exactly what to do, and then took me home to tell Mom. I am so thankful that Dad is okay. I was so confused for a few weeks, which seemed like years. Dad wasn't home, and it seemed like Mom would leave me alone all day. Grandma did come and stay for a while, which is always nice because she comes equipped with nonstop treats. A treat if I go outside, a treat if I come back in, etc. It's the best.

When I think back on the whole experience, people always talk about making lemonade out of lemons, or something silly like that; but that is exactly what happened. Due to some recent trouble I had gotten myself into, I was walking on pretty thin ice about the time this happened to Dad. I'm pretty sure that this life-saving effort earned me enough brownie points for life. When I say "brownie," I do mean "brownie," but more about that later.

CHAPTER TEN

THREE PIZZAS
& THE EASTER HAM

Roughly four months after saving Steve, my sister, Lynn, was kind enough to let us bring Cooper to her house, two hours away, in the Quad Cities on Easter. Her whole family loves dogs. My brother-in-law, John, is amazing with dogs and always spends quality time with Cooper when in town. She quickly agreed to let us bring him, but I was leery from the start. About fifteen minutes into our visit, he started "marking" all the plants in her house. Lynn didn't just have one or two plants, but Cooper quickly counted ten to twenty plants—all of which needed to be notified that he was there and in charge.

The next morning, my nephew, Andrew, had a morning soccer game. As I looked at her beautiful, scratch-free kitchen cabinets, I obviously didn't trust Cooper in the house alone while we were gone. We decided to put him in the garage. Let me point out, this is a HUGE, three-car, temperature-controlled garage. He was not being deprived; what could possibly go wrong?

Just a mere two hours later, we arrived back home with the intent to enjoy some leftover pizza for lunch. John opened the garage. I was in the car behind him, and he immediately motioned for me to join him. *Oh no*, I thought, *what did he do now?* I imagined destroyed soccer cleats or an empty bag of fertilizer. Instead, I walked in to see Cooper lying in the middle of the garage, perfectly satisfied in a bit of a food coma. He didn't even attempt to move and get up. Then, I looked next to him to see an endless mess of boxes and wrappers. Lynn and John have a large full-size refrigerator in their garage where they store drinks and large amounts of food that don't fit in the everyday refrigerator in the kitchen. The night before, they'd had a party, and there were three pizzas left over—the ones we had planned to have for lunch. Cooper, however, had other plans. While we were gone, he had opened the refrigerator and ate three large Harris Sausage Pizzas AND the Easter ham. Yes, the Easter ham. There was not a morsel of anything left except for the pizza boxes (and the little plastic tables that go in the middle). About the only thing he didn't do was crack open a cold Coors Light to go with it. That would've actually gotten him brownie points. One large Harris pizza is known to serve six humans, or—now, apparently, one Labrador retriever? I was furious. Not only did we not get to enjoy my favorite hometown pizza, but now I had to go pick up sandwiches for lunch and make a separate trip to the grocery store for another Easter ham. I was so sure no one would be at the store the day before Easter, and there would be plenty of ham!

You could almost see the pizza and ham inside Cooper's normally mighty but fit physique. The transformation from two hours earlier was incredible. His belly was now quite a bit rounder, and he almost looked like an expectant mother nine months into her pregnancy with triplets. He moved extremely slowly, groaning with each step. The look on his face was one of absolute misery, as though the end of the world was minutes away. I secretly took joy in his misery.

The most amazing thing was that, after all of this, Cooper never got sick. Steve and I got up hourly with him for the next twenty-four hours to take him outside, afraid he would get sick—but nothing! He was, however, a bit smelly on the three-hour car trip home. The only silver lining was that at least he looked despondent. It was more likely a combination of pain and guilt. Needless to say, I have never asked my sister if Cooper could join us on future trips to her home.

What really happened:

WHAT'S FOR DESSERT?

Journal entry, March 2013 (the day before Easter)

Let me set the record straight right off the bat. Mom first talks about me peeing all over Lynn's house. Who has plants all over INSIDE? I'm used to letting all of my friends know where I've been on my daily walks. I was just doing the same thing I always do. We don't have these living plants inside our home, why would anyone do that?

Now, regarding the pizzas and the ham, there's not much to say except that the smell was KILLING ME! They leave me all alone in a big scary garage with absolutely nothing to keep me occupied and no soft bed to sleep on, only a cold concrete floor. There was an amazing smell radiating out of the refrigerator, and I just couldn't help myself. Just imagine taking freshly baked chocolate chip cookies out of the oven and not being able to eat one, two... okay, all of them.

I only meant to have a piece of pizza, but then it tasted so good that I just couldn't help myself. Let me stop for a minute to educate everyone on the quality of this pizza. It is nothing like a typical cardboard frozen pizza. This is award-winning, original Quad Cities pizza—it cannot be beat! As I was taking the pizzas off of the shelves, there it was: a large, plump, Easter ham, just sitting there. I did actually pause to think about it for a few minutes and then settled on the argument that I was going to already be in trouble, so I might as well make it worth my while and eat the ham too. How much more trouble could I possibly get into? Of course, what they didn't do is give me credit for not breaking any glass. Do you realize how many bottles of beer and wine were in that refrigerator? I didn't even break one. I also didn't receive credit for figuring out how to open the refrigerator. Remember, I don't have hands and arms to pull it open. I was forced to use my mouth and teeth and wrap them around the handle and then back-up. It took several attempts, but after a while, I got the hang of it, and like magic, the door opened.

After they got home, they were yelling at me every hour to get up so they could take me outside to walk around. How ridiculous. After eating that much food, who wants to go for a walk? Hello, folks, can't you see I'm in a food coma and just want to lay here! In hindsight, thankfully this occurred three short months after I saved Dad and earned a lifetime of points accumulated on my card.

CHAPTER ELEVEN

TURKEY TROT CARB LOADING

Fast forward to Cooper's next visit with my family about seven months later. We hosted the entire Johnson clan for Thanksgiving. This meant 16 people staying at our house for the weekend. At first glance, it seemed overwhelming, but it was relatively easy to make room. We threw all of the kids into the basement and then divided up the bedrooms.

Cooper was thrilled. He loves when visitors come and stay. Not only are there plenty of young kids around who are ripe to steal from, but we are also distracted. We are not in our normal routine, which consists of monitoring Cooper's every move. It opens the door for food opportunities—figuratively and literally.

The day before everyone arrived, I had gotten two dozen bagels to eat before we all ran the annual 5K Turkey Trot. With sixteen people staying at the house, we had to be equipped with lots of bagels. My brother was the first to rise that morning. Or, should I say, the second. On his way downstairs, Eric tripped on an empty bagel box. The only other evidence was a few poppy and sesame seeds smashed into the carpet on the landing of the stairs. At some point during the night, Cooper—who didn't sleep in our room because of all of the family distractions—had gotten on the counter in the kitchen and stole all two dozen bagels. Actually, he ate twenty-six bagels because of the trusted baker's dozen. Once again, he never got sick. So, the one who did a carbo-load of epic proportions did not even run the 5K, while the rest of us had to leave early to make an extra stop at the bagel store on our way to the race.

What really happened

ALL YOU CAN EAT BAGELS

Journal entry, November 28, 2013

Once again, Mom isn't being fair. The entire day before, all everyone talked about was getting up early to run the Turkey Trot. How was I to know that I wasn't invited to run with them? I woke up extra early that morning to the smell of the bagels tempting me. I had heard somewhere that eating carbohydrates before a race is helpful. The part of the advice that I didn't quite catch was how many carbohydrates one should consume. The bagels were on the counter. As I grabbed one of the containers, the other accidentally fell over with it, so I figured that it wouldn't hurt anything.

Wow, was Mom ever mad at me and embarrassed. I overheard her ranting to Dad that I was making her look bad in front of her family again and started that "dog training" talk again. She's so sensitive, it was a few measly bagels—no big deal. She'll get over it, it's almost Christmastime, after all it's only been one year since I saved Dad.

CHAPTER TWELVE

NATIONAL DOG DAY

One typical school morning, in the fall of 2014, I left to drive the kids to school and to run a quick errand. I walked back into the house, a full thirty minutes later, to find a broken glass dish on the floor and an empty pan of brownies. Cooper had entered the kitchen and stole an entire pan of chocolate brownies and the eight buttermilk biscuits I had just baked to go with dinner. As everyone now knows, this was not the first time Cooper had stolen and eaten an extreme amount of food, BUT it was the first time he had consumed that much chocolate. Google had always told me that chocolate is poisonous to dogs, so this time I was actually worried. I immediately called the vet and began explaining what had happened. The receptionist also sounded quite worried; that is until she asked for my dog's name. Once she realized it was Cooper, her tone immediately changed, and it was suddenly much less of an emergency. As usual with Cooper's activities, he did not get sick at all. There was zero impact from the chocolate.

Later that same afternoon, I went to a meeting, and Cooper was once again left alone. Alex walked in from school to Cooper with the garbage can lid stuck on his head. Who knows how long it had been stuck on his head, but he was wandering around bumping into things until Alex kindly removed the lid for him. Not, however, before he captured the moment on camera.

That evening, while watching the evening news and preparing dinner, I learned that it was National Dog Day—

REALLY? What were the odds? Even I almost had to laugh. Then I glanced over at Cooper lying there. I swear he gave me a smug, I tried to tell you so, look. The kids and Steve enjoyed my story over dinner, learning that Cooper had helped himself to a treat to celebrate on his special day even though we had no brownies for dessert.

What really happened

MY FAVORITE HOLIDAY

Journal entry August 26, 2014

It is National Dog Day, so I just assumed they made the brownies for me. Later that afternoon, my stomach was a bit upset. I have no idea why, but those empty toilet paper rolls and tissues soothe me for some reason. I guess you can call them my version of Tums. I have to say, I was pretty embarrassed about the stupid garbage can lid. I usually can simply knock it off, but this time it got stuck on my head. I was helpless and had to wait for Alex to get home. I long for the days before social media. Of course, Alex had to snap a picture of me, which I will never live down.

CHAPTER THIRTEEN

CROUCHING TIGER, HIDDEN DRAGON

Before we had a Labrador retriever, I had always heard about what incredible hunting dogs they were. I was a bit hesitant, wondering if Cooper would cause trouble if he encountered any wildlife on our daily adventures in Michigan. Little did I realize that in this department, I had absolutely nothing to worry about.

One evening, Steve was walking Cooper when they came across a friendly neighborhood squirrel in the yard right in front of them. To say that the squirrel was afraid of the hundred-pound brown predator standing a short five feet in front of him could not have been more wrong. Everyone paused for just a moment, when all of a sudden, the squirrel charged directly toward them. The squirrel ran up and over Cooper as if he was a barricade on an obstacle course, and then continued up the tree on their left. It wasn't like the squirrel attacked; his route was simply the most direct and quickest route up the tree. Cooper didn't even flinch and kept walking as if nothing happened. I still laugh to myself when we see people on walks and a dog will frantically bark, pull, and yank, trying to vault up a tree after a squirrel. How in the world did that squirrel know that Cooper was zero threat?

As with squirrels, we also see rabbits in yards everywhere during walks. Cooper always walks by as if he doesn't even notice them. Once, when we lived in our old house on Newton Avenue, I looked out the front window while Cooper was lying in the front yard. A rabbit was calmly sitting about ten feet away from him and they were just staring at each other. This lasted for a good fifteen minutes, during which time neither of them moved.

In addition to squirrels and rabbits, Cooper is not phased in the least when he sees deer. In Michigan, we frequently get deer who graze and hang out in our yard. Cooper never even acknowledges the large creatures in his territory. I don't understand it, because whenever Cooper sees another dog on a walk, he immediately becomes a crouching tiger, hidden dragon. He squats down low and creeps slowly forward until he finally stops and lies down, staring intently, waiting for the dog to approach him. Cooper then jumps up and says hi. It doesn't matter if we're on the sidewalk, the park, or in the crosswalk in the middle of the street—his routine is the same.

What really happened

PSYCHO SQUIRREL

Journal entries summer of 2015

Okay—I have to admit, I am embarrassed about the squirrel. But let me provide you with a little bit of background. When I was a puppy, one night I had a nightmare about a psycho squirrel who attacked me. That night, I thought it was actually happening. It's not like me to get that skittish over a little thing like that, but just like sharks and snakes creep out my Mom, squirrels freak me out. I can't even look at them. I have also never understood those dogs that chase squirrels or bark at them when they run up the trees. Do they not know that there is no way in the world they are ever going to catch it? Most importantly, if I'm going to have a squirrel, I prefer mine medium-rare.

In regard to the bunny, I'm quite offended—I could never hurt a cute little rabbit. Have you NOT seen the movie Bambi with Thumper? He has my favorite quote of all time— "If you can't say nuffin' nice; don't say nuffin' at all!" I'm pretty social and am happy to share my yard with the friendly little bunny. Remember, Mom doesn't take me to the dog park anymore and typically crosses the street when one of my friends is approaching, so I have to take my socialization where I can get it and with whom I can get it from.

That brings me to Mom's "crouching tiger, hidden dragon" comment. Just when I think we're starting to understand each other, she says something silly like that. In reality, my behavior is quite polite, and this is simply my invitation to the oncoming dog for a playdate. You humans have things like Evite, but dogs do not. Whenever I lay down like that, I am simply telling my friend, "I want to play." Evite—the dog way.

CHAPTER FOURTEEN

COOPER THE LIFEGUARD

It took us a couple of years, but we finally broke down and let Cooper hang with us on our new floating dock. When the kids jump off the dock and swim to the ladder, Cooper always goes crazy, thinking they're drowning, and tries to save them. He starts barking excessively, then runs over to the ladder, trying to grab them by the life jacket to pull them up, and then licks them all over as they try to walk up the ladder.

Cooper has created his own game called "Spot the Flop." Along with the drip-dry and no-running on the dock rules, Steve has passed a "no-shoes on the boat" rule that people actually obey. Before getting on the boat, everyone kicks off their flip flops on the large floating dock platform and hop on the boat. Cooper barks and whines as we pull away, but as soon as he realizes his antics are not working, he grabs a shoe or two from one of the lucky boat goers and proceeds to hide it in the yard. He does not destroy the shoe. Perhaps he only makes a few minor bite marks on the foam flip-flop, but he makes his point that he one hundred percent disagrees with our decision to leave him behind. I suppose we could consider ourselves lucky that he doesn't drop it in the lake to float away with the current. He usually seems to target Steve or me. It's as if he knows whose shoes are whose, and who is responsible for the decision to leave him behind. It is his way of making a statement. We will yell at him, telling him to drop it; he will stop, turn around, give a little dog smirk, and keep walking.

Back to Fitzroy for a minute. He always loved laying calmly at the top of the hill watching all the surrounding activity. He didn't bark or steal shoes; instead, he gallantly laid there like royalty. After he passed, we had a grave marker made for him with a picture of him painted on a plaque with "Forever in our Hearts" written under it. We have it hanging on a tree next to where we buried his ashes. It's always a nice reminder of Fitz at his favorite place. Several years later; now, whenever Cooper is charging down the hill to cause chaos, he usually stops at the tree, right at the marker, and pees directly on Fitzroy's ashes and plaque. It is almost as if he knows he is there. That behavior is so incredibly annoying to me, yet eerily endearing.

Cooper has gotten quite used to the dock. It has become his absolute favorite place to be, other than the kitchen. Every year, we take annual photos with Steve's sister, Karen, and her husband, Paul, when they visit from New York. One year, we decided to take our annual family pictures on the boat with Karen, Paul, and the kids. It is always quite the production, taking pictures with both families—only the kids, the kids with grandma, etc. Cooper was sitting calmly and patiently on the dock that day, not causing any trouble. All of a sudden, it was our turn. Paul announced, "Purtells, you're up." Before anyone else moved, Cooper immediately jumped up and ran on the boat, front and center, for the picture. He had gotten skipped over time and time again, and it wasn't going to happen this year. As soon as we were done, he hopped off and ran off back up the hill to troll for any food left behind.

What really happened

SAVING THE CHILDREN

Journal entries from summer 2015 and 2016

They call it stealing shoes or "Spot the Flop," I prefer to say it's just my way of proving a point. It could be a lot worse, I could take both shoes, or drop the one I took into the lake, or chew them up. All I do is carefully pick my target, typically Mom or Dad for leaving me, then simply grab one of their shoes and go find a hiding place in the front yard. If I'm really mad, I'll do this a couple of times for more than one victim.

Since when do you not include the entire family in the family photo? I don't know how many times they've taken these pictures without me, and it wasn't going to happen again. I was patient and waited for my turn. When I heard Paul's signal, all I did was jump into action. I even smiled and looked at the camera. This year, I finally was included on the FRONT of the Christmas Card instead of the obligatory back, which I do realize is always an afterthought. You'd be eating brownies at 9 am if you were an afterthought too!

Lastly, I can't believe they don't appreciate the fact that I lifeguard for them. These poor kids are making all this noise and are in danger. I need to reach out to save them and help them up the steps. No one else is paying attention when the adults have those blue drinks. These kids make me so nervous with all of that screaming in distress. Thank goodness I'm finally allowed on the dock, or many could have drowned. I should get paid for this work, not scolded for it!

CHAPTER FIFTEEN

BAGGAGE CLAIM

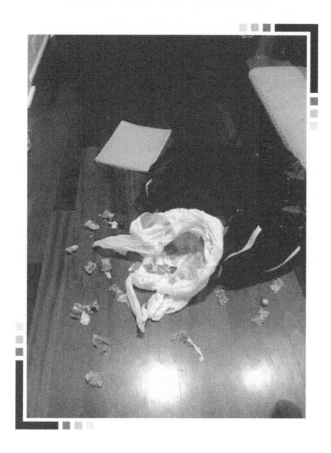

I've already hinted that Cooper had become quite the genius when it comes to opening bags; now for a couple of examples demonstrating his expertise. One evening, Madison had fifteen girls over for a soccer pasta party the night before a big game. The girls came over after practice, stormed in, and threw their backpacks on the floor in the entryway. One of the girls, Nora, was coming late, so the girls kindly put a plate of food aside for her. Even though I ordered enough for forty people, there was not a morsel left. When Nora arrived, the girls were handing Nora her plate when Cooper skillfully intercepted the food during the transition. His defense was something I'm sure he was proud of and could have been a great addition to the soccer team. Shortly after this play, I walked into the front room to grab something. All I saw was empty Ziploc bags all over the living room. Cooper had sniffed out the backpacks and carefully unzipped only the two that had food inside of them. He stole the food but nicely left the structure of the backpack undamaged, other than a little slobber around the zipper.

On another occasion, we were in Michigan for our friend, Jen's, 50th birthday celebration. It was a perfect, beautiful, sunny day in July. After spending the day on the lake, we went for a lovely dinner with a few close friends. A few hours later, we came home to find our other friend, Sherri's, United Airlines flight attendant luggage mysteriously unzipped. Sherri was working the next day and had packed herself some snacks for the flight. Her bag contained canned tuna and a protein bar placed in an inside hidden pocket. The problem was that there were so many compartments. Cooper unzipped the bag, but that didn't get him what he wanted. Unlike ever before, he did have to tear a small hole in the suitcase to get the food.

I have to give Cooper credit. Over the years, he has perfected his technique and no longer ruins the bag. He scopes out the alternatives and selects only the bags containing food. He then carefully unzips only the pocket containing the food. I have frequently thought that I needed to get him a dog sniffing job at O'Hare International Airport. He just might let the drugs go through, but not a morsel of that banned food!

What Really Happened

NINJA BAG OPENER

Journal entries fall 2015 & summer 2018

I mentioned when I was young that I've gotten myself into trouble over the years by ruining luggage or backpacks that contained food. By now, I have perfected my technique and don't ruin any inedible objects. I think Mom actually appreciates that fact. I also have to say that the United Airlines suitcase was NOT worth the effort. Canned tuna—YUCK! My tastes are much more refined than that. In the future, I will insist on Sushi Grade Tuna.

CHAPTER SIXTEEN

ONE FOOD COOPER WON'T EAT

Madison is very science-oriented and excels in pretty much everything she does; that is, everything except for cooking. One day when she was in middle school, she had an assignment to make pancakes for her food class. Thankfully, we weren't home to witness the mess or taste the result. Her response, when I asked about the pancakes, was, "Yeah, they weren't very good." About an hour later, she expanded on that comment and shared with me that she gave one to Cooper. He spit it out—WHAT? Cooper doesn't spit out anything. They must've been AWFUL!

After that experience, Madison stuck with simple things. Her specialties were frozen waffles, ramen noodles, Kraft Macaroni & Cheese, and chocolate chip cookies already in dough form that can be placed on the cookie sheet. One evening in the fall of 2018, just Madison and I were home for dinner. I decided to make bratwursts on the grill. I made the side veggie items and then had to take Alex to a friend's house. I asked Madison if she could please take off the brats when they were golden brown. My exact words were, something like, "They're almost done, so just take them off in about five minutes." I left with Alex and returned thirty minutes later as she was just taking them off the grill.

She said, "Mom, they took a lot longer than you thought, and I'm still not sure they're done."

"They're done," I replied while cringing a bit about this upcoming meal. We proceeded into the kitchen to make our plates. I reluctantly put my brat on a bun and loaded up my plate with salad and asparagus. I then bit into what tasted like my leather belt and tried not to make a face. I could not bring myself to take the next bite when Madison said, "Yeah, I think they're overdone, aren't they?"

"You think?" was my answer. I then promptly picked up the phone to order a pizza. I said, "Just give them to Cooper." Madison tossed her brat to Cooper, who is quite good at the mid-air food catch. He caught the brat but immediately dropped it, gave it a sniff, and walked away. Once again, Cooper doesn't spit out anything except for, apparently, Madison's pancakes and bratwursts.

What really happened

WORST COOK IN AMERICA

Journal entries spring 2014 and fall 2018

That girl is so talented, smart, funny, and beautiful, but holy cow, Madison can't cook for anything! First of all, let's talk about the pancakes. I was all excited when she started making them because no one else was home, and I knew she'd throw me the extras. She tossed it up in the air. So much for being "light and fluffy," this thing fell to the ground quicker than a bowling ball—THUD. I gave it the obligatory sniff and just had to walk away.

I was most disappointed, however, with the bratwurst. I didn't think you could screw those up. I'll eat them raw, perfectly cooked, or charred, but she managed to cook out every last bit of juice in the thing. I don't want to hurt her feelings, but I do believe that Dad's leather shoe, which I ate when I was a puppy, tasted better. She really might want to consider auditioning for Worst Cooks in America.

Don't get me wrong, Madison is pretty awesome. My favorite time to get in the garbage is when she's home because she cleans it up for me and I don't get in trouble. She's smart enough to know that Mom will not be happy. She covers for me all the time, and we have quite the bond.

CHAPTER SEVENTEEN

NEW HOUSE, NEW RULES

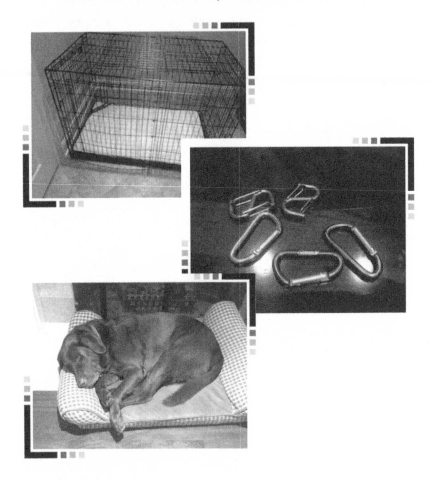

We were so excited to move. Our old house, on Newton, was a great place to first test out the suburbs after city living, and perfect for the kids when they were young. As the kids got a little older, we wanted to be closer to the schools and the center of uptown. At our house on Newton, Cooper was no longer allowed upstairs. He had peed all over every bedroom at some point during his six years, and we had invested in countless carpet cleanings. He had his comfortable dog bed that he was used to sleeping in on the main floor, and the Invisible Fence worked approximately eighty percent of the time, usually keeping the kitchen intact.

At the new house, we had to come up with a plan. Cooper couldn't be trusted alone on the main floor with its beautiful kitchen cabinets. We'd been down that rabbit hole before, and it felt mean to send him to the basement alone at night. Mind you, we are not talking about an unfinished creepy basement. It is a large, 1,000 square foot space with heated floors, a full bar, and a media room. A media room that Alex and his friends would never leave if they had the choice. I still can't believe our realtor, Jen, found the perfect house for us, and of course, Cooper! The basement is a true Cooper Palace. I'd be happy to be locked down there alone.

Finally, after much discussion, we had a plan. The good news for Cooper was that we decided to lock him in the room with us at night with his very own, comfortable, Tempur-Pedic bed. From Google, I also bought him a brand-new, extra-large, escape-proof, metal crate with a plush dog mat for the basement. He finally got to sleep in the room with us at night—yes, he was starting to grow on me, Easter ham and all.

When we were gone during the day, though, it was the basement for Cooper. The first time we came home after leaving him, there was drool all over the floor. He had been trying to get out of the crate and was exhausted, but he was still in the crate. "It might take him a few times, but he'll get used to this. It's going to work," I naively told Steve. The second time, Cooper escaped the crate and met us at the door. "Really? How did that happen? I must've not locked it correctly. It has got to be a fluke." The third time, Cooper escaped again and met us at door. This time, I also found a bone on the couch (that he is not supposed to be on). If ever I questioned whether he could be left alone now that he was six years old, the answer was a definite NO. As I went to investigate, I noticed that the crate was slightly mangled and bent. I can't believe he got out of this crate three times, it was the most "dog-proof" crate I could find after much Google research (Google said so!). The fourth time we left him, I upped my game and used four metal carabiner locks that I found at Home Depot to secure the crate. Once again, we came home to drool all over the floor, but he was still inside, and I was now feeling confident that this was going to work. The fifth time, I again used the four metal mountain climber locks. I began to realize that I was going to have to plan our departures to allow enough time to attach the locks to the crate. This was a pain and quite time-consuming.

That evening, a very proud Houdini Cooper escaped and met us at the door—WHAT? How in the world did he do this? What I should've done at this point is invest in a nanny cam for my dog; but if I had done that, I would already be a millionaire from the video going viral and probably would not be writing this book.

Upon further investigation, we found disfigured and broken metal clips, along with a lot of drool, all over the basement floor. To add insult to injury, we also had garbage all over the kitchen floor where he had helped himself in our new kitchen. Words cannot describe the anger that raged within me. It was right up there with when he peed on my bed, but he was now six years old. He was no longer a puppy—no excuses! Remember, I reminded myself, he saved Steve (which saved Cooper). I immediately put him outside, where he turned his back to me and just waited. I realized it was time to change my strategy. A Cooper-Proof crate does not exist.

During this entire time, I firmly believe that Steve and the kids were secretly, and at times non-so-secretly, laughing and rooting for Cooper in this mind game. "That's okay," I said, "I can always attach a baby gate to the stairs. There's no way he'll be able to jump over that on the stairs. He'll have free reign of the basement, but that's okay. We don't leave any food down there, so we're safe," I told myself. Yes, I was also now talking to myself.

The sixth time, I attached the extra-long baby gate to the stairs, about halfway up, so he couldn't jump over it. I made sure it was tightly fastened so he couldn't knock it over. I then confidently walked out. A few hours later, Cooper again met me at the door, this time with a mangled bag from a recently devoured loaf of bread hiding in the bathroom. If I remember right, I think I literally cried at this point. I actually had a dog that was smarter than me, and I was so frustrated. "He saved Steve, he saved Steve," I kept repeating.

I decided to make one additional attempt with the baby gate. "Maybe if I tied the gate to the metal spindles on the stairs, that would make it impossible for him to knock the gate over?" I also made sure to connect the Invisible Fence unit in the kitchen so even if he escaped, he could not enter the kitchen. Sure enough, about three hours later, a proud brown beast met me at the door. This time, he had untied the rope, but he had not gone in the kitchen. Wait, I had an epiphany—I can move the indoor Invisible Fence unit to the stairs in the basement!

That night, I made sure to fully charge the indoor unit. The next morning, I told Cooper to "kennel up" and he immediately ran downstairs into the open crate. The crate was never the problem, only because he always gets a treat every time he complies. I then went and got the Invisible Fence unit and placed it on the landing of the staircase. I simply propped the baby gate up in front of it. What I didn't share with Cooper was that a light breeze of wind could have easily knocked it over. "Be good," I said, and Cooper and I had a lengthy stare-down moment. I was cautiously optimistic this approach would work, but I was sure he couldn't wait for me to leave so he could see how long it would take him to complete his puzzle of the day.

YES, the eighth time was the charm! I came home, and he was anxiously waiting for me at the bottom of the basement stairs, baby-gate still intact. FINALLY! Cooper had won several battles, but I finally won the war. Four years later, this is still our routine. I also need to share a secret with you. Two years ago, I stopped putting the Invisible Fence unit on the staircase. He now associates the baby gate with the beep and won't go anywhere near it—shhhh he still hasn't figured that one out. He's smart but I'm still smarter.

What really happened

THE HAUNTED BASEMENT

Journal entry spring of 2015

How many movies have you seen with haunted basements? I can't believe they think they're going to leave me down there. They keep bragging and going on and on about how this Jen person found us the perfect house. I'd like Jen to see just how perfect it is in this crate all day. I had the old house all figured out, now I need new tricks. I already proved that I'm smarter than your typical dog crate. Now they've gotten sneaky and invested in the "extra-secure" crate (that Mom Googled, there's the silly human word again). Let's just see about that. I was a bit embarrassed. The first time, I couldn't get out. Oh well, I'll just give them a false sense of security. The second time, I was out in thirty minutes flat and had the whole house to myself. This was quickly becoming an awesome game that I play with Mom. She puts me downstairs, gives me a treat, and leaves. That's when the game starts. It is so much fun. I usually win but, every once in a while, I let her win. The false sense of security is kind of nice.

I was winning the game when all of a sudden, that darn Kryptonite entered the picture. There is nothing worse than that hair-raising "beep, beep, beep" noise. How did they put Kryptonite into a baby-gate? The inventor of that is a true genius. There is nothing more terrifying! Over time, I've come to realize that the basement isn't so bad. It's cold down there, and I always get a treat before they leave. Once again, not ideal, but I'll survive. It's also not so bad not getting in trouble all of the time. Mom and I are bonding more and more these days.

CHAPTER EIGHTEEN

FORGET ME NOT

One benefit of moving to our new house is that Cooper now lives a block away from his sister, Reece. His sister is about half the size of Cooper, but equally in love with food. Over the years, together with Reece's owners, we've shared many stories about the food-loving siblings.

Daily walks are also never boring with Cooper. I remember one day we were going for a nice stroll past several local businesses, one of which was Nonno Pino, a local Italian restaurant. It was early morning before the restaurant opened but after a morning delivery. There was a bag full of Italian bread outside their door. I didn't realize this fact until Cooper nonchalantly grabbed a loaf. He kept walking with the two-foot-long loaf hanging out of his mouth for about sixty seconds until he was able to gulp it down. Horrified, I quickly increased my speed and subsequently changed my route.

Walks in the winter months after it snows are Cooper's favorite because so many people put out leftover bread for the birds. He sniffs it out a couple of houses away and somehow always knows it's there. We walk by, and he immediately lunges forward to grab it before I even realize what's going on—poor birds.

One day, Steve and I were leaving to watch one of Alex's swim meets, and I verbally asked Madison to take Cooper for a walk while we were gone. He heard us and started pacing back and forth near her, knowing that she was supposed to take him. A few hours passed, and Madison continued watching Netflix, or whatever else teenage girls do in their rooms, and forgot to take him. But she failed to mention that to me.

Later that night, as I was bringing some clean clothes into her room, I noticed a big yellow puddle. He had peed in her room! I quickly began yelling at Cooper and shoved him outside. "Bad dog!" He took the punishment in stride, as he always does. When Madison came home that evening, as usual, she came into our room to talk to Cooper. He promptly turned his head away from her when she tried to pet him and wouldn't even look at her. That is when she confessed to me that she had forgotten to walk him. Cooper knew that she was supposed to take him for a walk, but Madison hadn't followed through, so he was getting his revenge by peeing in her room. I have to give him a little credit for finally taking his revenge out on someone other than me. Even though it was me who had to clean up his mess, I did have to chuckle at how he targeted her. Smart dogs really might be over-rated.

What really happened

DON'T YOU FORGET ABOUT ME

Journal entries 2015-2018

Let me start by talking about how great my winter walks are, especially after new-fallen snow. People must feel bad that I have to walk outside in bare feet, so they toss their leftover bread onto the snow for me. I really can't get over how nice people are. I just can't figure out why they don't do that in the summer? I must also chime in about the lottery I hit that one morning walking past that restaurant. I hit the jackpot, a whole loaf of fresh Italian bread. It was even still warm. So delicious! The hardest part was gulping it down before Mom grabbed it away from me. It's not like I could return the bread. She might as well just let me enjoy it.

There is nothing worse than when someone doesn't follow through with something they promise to do. That is exactly what Madison did today. I was so excited because she normally gives me long walks, sometimes even in the forest preserve. She was so busy watching "The Office" that she couldn't spare just a little bit of time to take me. It's not like she wasn't reminded. I can be very persistent and reminded her time and time again. When I thought she was going to take me, she just hopped in her car and left when her friend, Carley, came over. I was furious! At least she forgot to put me downstairs. When I initially went into her room, I was just browsing to see if she had any good snacks—denied again, nothing. I wasn't going to do it, but just couldn't help myself, I had to let her know what she did. Mom will never find out because Madison will feel guilty and clean it up. At least she'd know what she did. How was I to know this was laundry day?

CHAPTER NINETEEN

NO SUCH THING AS COOPER PROOF

Having a dog like Cooper, I needed to research the best food container to store dog food in the new house. Unlike our other home, we no longer had a spot in the Invisible Fence proof kitchen to store it, so the container would be kept in the mudroom. Therefore, we needed it to be dog-proof. Keeping up with the tradition of research, I went to Google and found the "Vittles Vault" with the following description: "a spinning lid to lock in freshness and lockout pets." Perfect, this is exactly what we needed. Problem solved. I immediately purchased the highest-rated "dog-proof" food container. Over time, we noticed small bites on top of the food container, but he was unable to crack the code.

Yes, once again, I spoke too soon. Cooper had been behaving himself for quite a while, and I had to leave for just about two hours, so I decided to leave him upstairs. We had the Invisible Fence, a circle of fear, so he couldn't get into the kitchen. What could possibly go wrong? That afternoon, when I returned home, Cooper ran past me without acknowledgment. As previously mentioned, that is always a bad sign. The kitchen was all clear, it seemed the Invisible Fence had done its job. I then walked into the living room and found the previously full Vittles Vault empty and mangled, with small chewed up plastic pieces all over the floor. The container had been almost full, with approximately twenty pounds of Natures Balance dog food inside. Now it was empty. As happened before, he once again had zero side effects, except for maybe a few more bathroom trips in the following hours.

What really happened

I'M SMARTER THAN GOOGLE

Journal entries 2016-2018

One of my favorite things to do is prove people wrong. I get so tired of Mom bragging that they had finally found a "dog-proof" food container. I had been eyeing it for a while because, after all, I am watching every night when they open it for dinner. It didn't look too difficult, after all. You're looking at Houdini, who can get out of cages with metal clasps (*even those made to hold the weight of a full-grown person*). I took a couple of sample attempts, but when opportunities arose, the container was always close to empty and not worth my time. So, I waited. Patiently. Today, I was super hungry, and they weren't home at 4:00 pm—dinner time, so I decided to help myself. Piece of cake. Just push down, twist, and turn. I tried to tell Mom that I was sorry I made a slightly larger mess than I anticipated. The plastic had seen better days and was no longer usable; BUT I was no longer hungry. Most importantly, I wasn't going to starve to death. Once again, I think I might have slightly misjudged the correct portion size. Oh well, maybe next time I'll get it right. Once you have one potato chip, you may as well eat the whole bag—right?

CHAPTER TWENTY

JOHN THE DOG SITTER

John Michaels has been our dog sitter for over ten years. He started watching Fitzroy, who, like us, was always his favorite ("perfect" dog). John was amazing. He would drive over to pick up Fitz and take him to his house while we were gone. I think Fitz used to even sleep in his bed with him, a practice that thankfully we've never adopted. Once Cooper came along, we approached John about also taking Cooper. "Sure," was his immediate reply. Before the first visit, we gave Cooper many lectures about not ruining it for us. I was a nervous wreck the entire trip. If Cooper blew this for us, we were in major trouble. Neither dog was fond of crates— you've already heard about Cooper's feelings about staying in them. Thankfully, Cooper behaved himself, because, from that point forward, John began watching both dogs. And after Fitzroy crossed over the Rainbow Bridge, he continued to watch Cooper for us any time we asked. John is marvelous with the dogs. Cooper gets so excited whenever his white van drives up. So much so that, at times, when we return from our trip, Cooper runs back outside and jumps in his van. It might have something to do with the fact that John is a musician and plays his guitar to Cooper and takes him on numerous walks a day.

In ten years, we never got a call from John about Fitzroy. But now, every time the phone rings when we're out of town, I get nervous because Cooper is very much a different breed. I equate it to getting a behavioral discipline call from the principal or teacher at school. I'm lucky to have never received one of those calls regarding my children. Calls regarding my dog, on the other hand, I'm not so lucky. John insists that most of the time Cooper behaves himself. He claims the most he ever took was a loaf of bread left on the counter. I'm not quite sure we believe that, but we will go with it; after all, he continues to watch him. John used to always take him to his house and even to his parent's home on holidays. I don't even take him to my own parent's home on holidays because he can't be trusted.

One Thanksgiving, when John was watching Cooper at our house, I received a call from John that he had mistakenly forgotten to put the Kryptonite baby gate up and had left for twenty minutes. When he got home, Cooper had opened up his "snack cabinet" and eaten an entire year supply of heartworm medicine. Frantically, John contacted the vet who assured him he will be okay. The following week, I refilled his medicine. About three weeks later, I decided to "trust him" for a quick errand and returned home to his large container of fifty, large, Milk-Bone Dog biscuits and another year's supply of heartworm pills completely gone. So, in two months, Cooper ate a two-year supply of heartworm medicine with ZERO side effects. I no longer felt guilty about forgetting to give it to him the previous month.

WHAT HAPPENS ON VACATION, STAYS ON VACATION

Journal entries 2015-2018

Who wouldn't love someone who over-feeds me, sits and plays the guitar to me all night, and takes me on countless walks throughout the day? John is the absolute best! I no longer get upset when my family deserts me on vacations because I too get pampered. Shhhh, don't tell Mom, because I still pretend to be mad when I see the suitcases come out. It's fun to make them feel guilty.

I also very much appreciate the bond that John and I have. Trust me, I've managed to get plenty of treats under his watch that he doesn't share with Mom. "What happens on vacation, stays on vacation." The other thing is that, because he is very generous with his feedings, I'm not starving all of the time and don't always have to help myself. He gets me, he really gets me!

Let me just describe a typical evening with John. After a generous dinner, we go for a long walk. Did I point out this is typically the third or fourth long walk of the day? Sometimes I'm really lucky and he brings some of his other dog friends along with him. Then we retreat to the family room where he breaks out his guitar and plays for hours and hours. It's so relaxing, and I just cuddle up by him and enjoy the music.

CHAPTER TWENTY-ONE

"FAST" FOOD

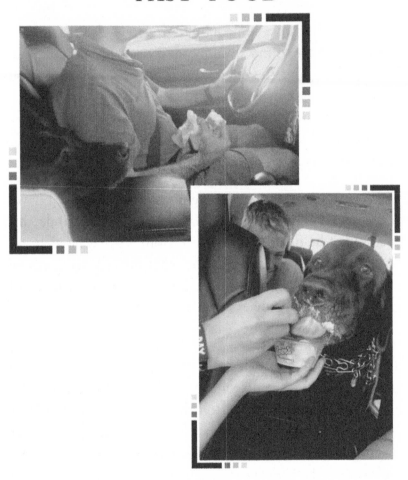

I mentioned before that, throughout the years, Cooper was known for snatching a burger or two, or ten, from unsuspecting passengers on our drives to Michigan. After several 'burglaries,' we finally gave in and started buying Cooper a burger on our trips. To be perfectly honest, I started feeling guilty that he had to sit in the car and smell the food. What harm can a burger do?

The kids loved Steak-N-Shake fries and mini-sliders, and there was one right on the way with a drive-through. We stopped there frequently on our drives. The first time we ordered Cooper a burger, he was so happy and didn't even bother to wait for the kids to unwrap it—GULP! It was gone in a matter of three seconds. The next time we hit the drive-through, I again ordered Cooper his plain hamburger. As we were driving away, we realize that everyone got their food except for Cooper! Oops, out of all the people to forget, he was NOT very understanding. The line was extremely long, and this mistake did not warrant a return trip to fix the error. Alex immediately jumped in to defend his pal and offered him one of his mini sliders. Shockingly, the next time we stopped there; the same thing happened. What are the odds? Poor Cooper was denied again! Frustrated and getting harassed by the kids for not going back, I reluctantly pulled into a Culver's across the street to order another plain hamburger for Cooper. I was annoyed because I'm one of those drivers who does not like to stop on road-trips. This is something I inherited from my father who would never let us place a "special order" on a road trip when going to a drive-through because it would take too long. The only stops were gas stops, and you had better be quick. I still vividly remember my brothers peeing in a Coke can on long road trips because it was not yet time for gas.

Back to the Culver's experience. When I pulled up to receive Cooper's burger, he impatiently stuck his huge brown nose out the window as if to grab it himself. The nice woman said, "Ahhh he is so cute, would the puppy-like an ice cream?" Are you kidding me—they have doggie ice cream? Oh well, I had no choice than to say yes with the kids begging. I have to admit, it was so cute to watch him inhale his ice cream and burger with such a look of satisfaction. Since then, we have not made a repeat visit to Steak-N-Shake with Cooper in the car—Culver's is king!

What really happened

THE MAGIC WINDOW

Journal entry, summer 2017

Let me start by saying that I love car rides. I'm never quite sure where I'm going, but if they all have suitcases, and I get to go, that always means Michigan. Almost every time that means going through a magic window during the adventure. I've now mastered the ability to, as I call it, "distract and grab." Madison and Alex are pretty good at maintaining control, but it's awesome when they have friends. Here is the one problem that I have. They always want to go through the Steak-n-Shake magic window, which is the worst place ever. Now that I've trained my family to order me a burger too, I get upset if it doesn't happen. The problem is that on two different occasions, they ordered me a plain hamburger, and those mean people did not give us that part of the order. The first time, Alex gave me one of his—but understand, that meant I got a small one instead of one large burger. It barely even constituted a snack. That's like one M&M for me. The next time, they went across the street and drove through a Culver's, or as I refer to it, THE BEST RESTAURANT EVER! Not only did they give me my burger, but they even asked, "Would the pup like ice cream?" Are you kidding me, finally a restaurant that understands me? Of course, I want ice cream! Mom also even played along and let me have it. She really does understand me.

CHAPTER TWENTY-TWO

THE CASE OF THE MISSING CLIFF BARS

One afternoon, Madison had several girls from the cross-country team over for pizza. As one of them arrived, she met the UPS man at the door, and he handed her a package. Madison's friend placed it on the bench in the front entryway where everyone puts all the delivery packages.

Oversight #1: No one looked at the name and address on the package.

Steve, Alex, and I had already left for Panino's Italian Restaurant to enjoy dinner and a glass of wine. I'm estimating we were gone for two hours.

Oversight #2: When Madison and her friends left, she forgot to put Cooper downstairs.

When we arrived back home after dinner, there was a torn brown envelope, and remnants of light blue, bright purple, and bright red wrappers all over the floor. Shockingly, Cooper quickly brushed by us and ran outside. He had opened the package containing an entire case of Cliff Bars. That is eighteen Cliff Bars. I was so confused; we had not ordered the Cliff Bars. Why did they deliver them to us, and who's were they? One would never know because Cooper had also conveniently eaten that part of the envelope.

Like most of Cooper's antics, I posted a photo of the mangled package and remaining wrappers on Facebook, only to have my friend and neighbor located a few houses down respond, "Now I know what happened to my Cliff Bars!" I was horrified and promised to repay her in wine.

Fast forward three days. I was walking Cooper when he started hobbling around in circles and preparing to do his business. He was taking much longer than normal and seemed to be in real pain. Finally, after he did his business, I saw all of the colors of the rainbow and zero fecal matter. It was only mangled bright red, blue, and yellow plastic. I should feel bad for him, but it serves him right. Maybe now he'll learn?

What really happened

UNABLE TO RETURN TO SENDER

Journal entry, fall 2017

First of all, I had good intentions. I had barked at the UPS man, trying to tell him it wasn't our package, but he didn't listen. After everyone left, I was reading the label because I was concerned about the package getting to its intended owner. Then I smelled it. I'd had a long walk earlier that day and needed some protein, so I just couldn't resist opening it and tasting one. After that, they were so good, I couldn't help myself. Crunchy oats sprinkled with tasty chocolate chips. I'm sure I'm not the only one who struggles to stop eating once I start. Oops, Mom is going to be mad, but it's not our package, so maybe she won't even notice? I tried to hide the evidence by eating the wrappers too, but they weren't gone long enough. Let me tell you, I did learn my lesson. That really hurt after the fact. It was a three-day hangover. From now on, I'm unwrapping them first.

CHAPTER TWENTY-THREE

SALAMI AND THE LILYPAD

It was a beautiful July weekend, and we had invited our friends, the Rourkes, up to Michigan for the weekend. The boys were obsessed with catching a massive, extremely ugly, garfish off of the dock. That season, Alex and his friends had hooked him several times, but each time, he managed to flop off the line. This morning, we were out of bait, and they resorted to being creative. They were rummaging through the refrigerator and, unbeknownst to me, they grabbed some mini salami pieces. Immediately after putting the salami on the line, the fish bit again, but again escaped. (Why is this important? Wait until the end of the chapter and you will find out).

Like most sunny summer days in Michigan, we spend a lot of time taking the kids tubing, skiing, and wakeboarding in the afternoon. This is Cooper's least favorite time of the day because we leave him barking and howling on the dock. He will eventually give up, take a shoe, and head back to the house. This time was different. Alex was midway through his wakeboard ride when my phone started ringing. It was Liz, my next-door neighbor. I almost didn't pick up, thinking that I'd just call her later. But she usually texted and rarely called, so it must have been important.

"Hello?" A panicked Liz on the other end of the phone screamed that she saw Cooper fall off the dock. He couldn't get out, so he's swimming after us in the middle of the lake toward the boat. Meanwhile, the lake was full of tubers, skiers, kayakers, and wave runners. Now, apparently, a large brown blob was also swimming straight down the middle of the lake like he was on a suicide mission.

I replied, "Thank you, I'm on my way." I then abruptly stopped the boat to grab Alex, who had just gotten up for one of his first times on the wakeboard. Way to go Alex, but let's go! After Alex jumped back in the boat, with no time to drip dry (sorry Steve), we sped off to the other side of the lake where we saw Cooper heading toward us. As we arrived, Liz's college-age children, Madison and Noah, also reached him on their wave runners and were trying to shelter him from other boats. Cooper saw us and immediately swam toward the boat. This time he was quick to let Steve pull him up the ladder onto the boat. Panting and exhausted after having just swum about a half of a mile, Cooper was happy and finally satisfied that he got his boat ride.

Afterward, we were all perplexed as to how he fell off the dock into the weeds, a section of dock that he runs down a hundred times a day, every day, every summer without falling in. The mystery was soon solved when Steve grabbed his collar to bring him into the house for a "timeout" for bad behavior. Cooper stopped walking in the same spot where our neighbor said he fell in and again leaned over the dock. Steve looked into the water and soon located the culprit. Only slightly larger than the size of a quarter was a perfectly round piece of salami lying in the middle of a lily pad a couple of feet away from the dock. Cooper had sniffed out the salami as he walked back toward the house, leaned over, and fell in trying to snag it.

What really happened

EPIC FAIL

Journal entry, summer 2017

The boys were fishing all morning and didn't share any of the salami with me. In fact, they made me stay inside and wouldn't even let me help them. Later in the afternoon, after getting deserted again on the dock, I was lucky enough to smell some on my way back up to the house. I leaned over, almost got it. OH NO! Too far… SPLASH, I fell in.

Let me explain something to those who haven't been to our place in Michigan. We aren't talking about a nice sandy beach bottom here. Our dock is long for a reason. We have a big mucky swamp in the shallow part of the lake.   I'm embarrassed to admit it, but my big body can only lean so far before the laws of gravity take over. There were SO MANY weeds, and no way I was going to walk through the muck and weeds to the shore. That's disgusting! I wanted to be with everyone on the boat anyway, and I'm a good swimmer; so, I thought I'd go find my family. Darn, I never did get the salami. I'll have to chalk this up as an epic fail on my part.

CHAPTER TWENTY-FOUR

GARRETTS POPCORN, DELIGHTING CUSTOMERS SINCE 1949

After her sophomore year in high school, Madison came home from spending two weeks at a Northwestern University seminar for high school students interested in entering the medical profession. During her two weeks, she enjoyed her freedom. She spent many days taking the train into Chicago. On one of those visits, she purchased a tin of Garrett Popcorn. For those of you not lucky enough to have ever tried Garrett Popcorn, it is amazing. Every batch is handmade throughout the day, resulting in continuous, long lines outside their shops regularly, year after year. Our favorite popcorn is the Garrett Mix, which is a blend of CaramelCrisp and CheeseCorn. My father, who lives three hours from Chicago, has been known to put in special requests before I make a trip back to visit. Madison brought it home in a sealed metal container and was planning on bringing it to Michigan with us that weekend as a surprise for my father who was coming to visit. We were leaving the next morning. Since we were leaving in the morning, Madison left her suitcase in the entryway with the sealed metal container inside. Knowing the popcorn was in her bag, I warned her that she better take it out and keep in the kitchen until we leave because Cooper WILL eat it. Madison replied, "Mom, it's in a sealed, metal container in my suitcase; it will be fine!" She was then off to cross country practice. Okay then...

I subsequently left to take Alex to a friend's house and was gone for approximately fifteen minutes. When I came home, Cooper again skipped the meet-and-greet and immediately ran outside, but I was so busy getting ready to head out of town that I did not pay attention. That is UNTIL I walked into the front room. Madison's suitcase was open, and on the floor in the living room was a mangled empty, now "un-sealed," metal, Garrett Popcorn tin. I was gone for fifteen minutes!

This time I didn't even bother to get mad at Cooper. Madison did this to herself. I had even issued her a warning. I simply took out my phone, snapped a photo, texted her the photo with a sarcastic comment about the "sealed container," and then diligently logged it into my list of Cooper stories. I'm beginning to appreciate Cooper's sense of humor and personality.

What really happened

GARRETTS POPCORN, DELIGHTING ME TODAY

Journal entry, fall 2017

Aren't you hungry just listening to Mom describe the fresh, mouth-watering popcorn? Believe me, words don't even begin to do it justice, it almost melts in your mouth. It was delicious! As much as I love Madison, she deserved this one. Mom even warned her that I would help myself; but she chose to be lazy and not listen. I equate it to the "dog-proof" container. If someone tempts me, I am always up for the challenge. I am also getting wise in my middle-aged years. The suitcase was not even damaged, and the "sealed" container was an absolute joke. It took a whole thirty seconds to have the tin open so I could enjoy the legendary popcorn that has been delighting customers since 1949. I must say, they did not disappoint. The best part about it was I don't think that Mom was very mad at me. Madison took the brunt of this one. We really are beginning to understand each other.

CHAPTER TWENTY-FIVE

PADDLEBOARDING ANYONE?

In the spring of 2017, we purchased two new paddleboards that I immediately fell in love with. There is nothing better than waking up in the early morning with the steam rising off the lake. It's like glass, not a ripple in sight. I paddle around the lake before all the boaters come out for the day and create those annoying waves. The paddleboards get a lot of use. Guests always take them out for a spin. The kids, in a group of six or seven, sometimes caravan with the tube around the lake. It entertains them for hours as they stop at the park on the other side of the lake and then argue about who has to paddle and who gets to go along for the ride. The entire time they are gone, lifeguard Cooper always stands watch on the dock, patiently awaiting their return, at which time he begins to howl excessively and annoys everyone around him.

Cooper too was intrigued by this new toy that everyone was enjoying so much and wanted to get in on the fun. One day, as my friend Beth and I floated by the dock on the paddleboard, we started discussing how we thought Cooper would enjoy a ride. We subsequently coaxed Cooper onto the board. It was easier than I thought it would be. Cooper enjoyed his ride and stood very stately as we swam the board around the lake for about ten minutes.

What really happened

NEW PROFILE PIC

Journal entry, spring of 2017

Really, all I'm trying to do is relax on the dock, and they shove me onto this floating board. I can't walk around, lie down, or even move. Mom thinks I look "stately." Boy is she ever wrong, I'm simply terrified. This is no fun at all. After the fact, I do have to admit that it did result in a pretty awesome photo opportunity. I'm thinking about making it my profile picture on Facebook.

CHAPTER TWENTY-SIX

SCHOOL ADMISSIONS TEST

I've always had a passion for organizations that help school-age children read. During a search for an organization where I could volunteer, I found an amazing organization called "SitStayRead." This is a Chicago-based not-for-profit organization that brings dog teams and volunteers into low-income Chicago public elementary schools to help improve literacy skills. This was perfect. Not only could I volunteer and help the kids, but I could also try to get Cooper certified so he could join me! He would be ideal for this. He loves little kids and will gladly put up with anything that first or third graders can dish out as long as he gets attention and the occasional treat.

I attended an initial meeting to find out what was involved for Cooper and me to get certified. I immediately fell in love with the organization, the people, and their mission. I needed to first attend some training and observation sessions but, at first glance, I thought Cooper could pass this test.

I received the details on what exactly they look for in a "Dog Team" dog. The trainer went through the entire test with us, question by question. Sit, stay, down—check; gets along well with other dogs—check; can handle loud distractions—check; will sit calmly in a loud environment—check; not distracted by open food—Houston we have a problem! I raised my hand and asked the instructor "Is the open food part a deal-breaker? Because I guarantee he will take it."

She laughed and responded, "Oh no, we're primarily looking for good-tempered dogs." Phew, we should be okay, but we would have to practice.

I brought the sample test home and shared it with everyone. I then put Madison and Alex to work for daily practice with Cooper. I must say that Cooper likely gained about ten pounds in the next couple of weeks because he received many treats each time he followed commands and behaved properly.

Test day had arrived, and it was time for me to take Cooper downtown for his test. The test was from 6:30-7:30 pm, so I decided to leave extra early so we could go for a long walk in Lincoln Park to wear him out. As soon as we got out of the car, at about 5:00 pm, it was a new environment, and Cooper was pulling me in every direction, acting crazy, and reaching to play with every dog he saw. I was a nervous wreck and came very close to hopping back in the car and going home. This was going to be a disaster.

Suddenly, it was 6:30 pm, and we were waiting patiently at the front door for Victoria and the dog whisperer to arrive for his test. We were first inside to set up with our blanket. Another dog and his owner soon arrived, and, surprising to me, Cooper didn't even flinch or pull to say hello. He calmly wagged his tail and laid down. We began to go through each task, which he performed "perfectly." Next up was the food distraction, I grabbed his leash extra firmly and begin to walk around the food. I couldn't believe it. He didn't pull at all;

instead, he strutted past the food and then back to our home base. I almost checked to make sure I had the correct dog because he was so "perfectly" behaved. How had I doubted him earlier? Soon after the test was over, Cooper received his diploma and passed his test with flying colors. It was as if my child had just gotten accepted to the college of their dreams. I was so proud! I couldn't wait to get back to the car so I could text Steve and the kids to share the happy news. During our three-block walk along Clark Street, I kept talking to Cooper and telling him what a good boy he was. *I think I've been too hard on Cooper*, I was thinking. *He is such a good dog.*

On the way back to the car, we passed a cute little outdoor café. I was too focused on keeping Cooper from a dog I saw sitting a few tables down by his owner's side at the café. In a mastermind movement, with ease, he lunged sideways and grabbed a roll from the plate of an older handicapped woman sitting in a wheelchair! Yes, he took food from a handicapped woman. I was horrified and immediately began apologizing profusely. The woman and her table luckily were laughing hysterically. More than once, I offered to pay for their dinner, and she responded "No, no, honey. It's totally fine, I wasn't eating the bread anyway. Too many carbs; although, it doesn't seem to bother him any." I apologized for the tenth time, and we kept going on our way.

Cooper just looked at me—now he was proud.

What really happened

PASSED THE TEST: LETS "ROLL"

Journal entry, August 2018

Mom brought home the dog test and started reading the questions aloud to the family. They were all concerned that I wouldn't be able to pass because I couldn't resist the food. Valid concern—BUT, they forgot about how smart I am. This test is going to be a breeze: sit, stay, down, come, don't let distractions bother me, plays well with others, etc. Every day, Madison and Alex kept practicing over and over with me which was great because each time I did something right, I got a treat. What they didn't know was I had this down on day one, but the treats were so tasty, so why spoil their fun?

On the day of the test, I was so proud AND, if I do say so myself, I made Mom look like a rock star! I aced that test with no problem. Then came the walk to the car. I was hungry—after all, I had worked very hard and hadn't yet had dinner. Mom had the nerve to walk me past this outdoor café that smelled AMAZING—a place where the food is outside waiting for me! As I walked past, I couldn't help but spy the dinner roll, right on the edge of a plate of a woman who was deep in conversation with her friends. So, I snagged it. Big mistake, because I did not see she was in a wheelchair until it was too late. Even I admit that it wasn't very nice, and I was pretty horrified at myself. After Mom apologized, the woman insisted she wasn't going to eat it anyway so, no harm, no foul—and the roll was pretty tasty. The lady was right, carbs don't bother me. I guess I should be more cautious about selecting my victims.

CHAPTER TWENTY-SEVEN

COOPER GOES TO SCHOOL

We passed our Dog Team test in August, and it was a long wait until mid-October when the school sessions started. I have to admit, I was very much looking forward to attending school with Cooper. It would be a real bonding experience for both of us. The day was finally here! I pulled out a red and black drawstring bag and loaded it with a soft grey blanket, dog treats, hand sanitizer, and dog bags. The final step was Cooper's uniform, a blue work bandana that I tied around his neck. He wasn't quite sure what was going on, but I was getting his leash, so he was happy. He looked very proud of his blue bandana. He was a much more regal, serious Cooper. We jumped in the car and soon arrived at Brunson Math & Science Academy.

Upon arrival, we waited in front of the main entrance as instructed by Sarah, our Program Leader. She came out to get us. I asked if he could do a quick meet and greet outside with the other two dogs that were going to be in the classroom since this was his first time. However, that wasn't going to work since the other two dogs were already inside and ready. I was so nervous. We walked into the entryway and Cooper got a little too close. One of the dogs barked and lunged towards him. Oh no, I thought, we were going to get kicked out before we started. We came to find out that this dog was older and was wonderful with the kids but didn't care for new dogs stealing his spotlight.

The first time I walked in with Cooper, many of the kids gasped at his size, and all started waving at him. They took turns coming over to meet, pet, and read to him. Some kids ran right up and couldn't wait to start petting Cooper, but others were extremely tentative and scared at first. The best feeling was when they gained the courage to put out their hand for him to sniff. He responded with a big, sloppy kisses. That always got a laugh and took away any anxiety they might have. The most wonderful thing about this program is that you observe, first-hand, the drastic improvement in the kids' development. Children who are timid about reading, writing, or sharing their stories during the first few visits suddenly begin to write the most in-depth, imaginative, amazing stories by the fourth or fifth visit with Cooper. They can't wait to share their work with Cooper! The confidence that many of the children gain is so heart-warming and rewarding. My favorite story has to be from a little boy who every week wrote about Cooper the Wonder-Dog. Each week it was a different adventure that usually involved Cooper taking food, but then ultimately ended with him saving the day.

It only took Cooper one visit to figure out this school routine. From that point on, every time I grabbed that red and black drawstring bag and showed him his work bandana, he started jumping and howling. Cooper doesn't jump and howl, but he just can't contain his excitement when he sees his uniform.

Cooper and I very much enjoy our weekly school visits. In the winter, I received a flier advertising SitStaRead's annual dog-friendly fundraiser. Yes, I said dog-friendly fundraiser. I immediately saved the date and Googled "large dog tuxedo costumes." I think this might've been the most excited I have ever been for a fundraiser. "This was going to be awesome." I found a dog tuxedo for Cooper. I purchased an extra-large, but I can't say it was a perfect fit. He was busting out in the chest, but it worked. The day of the fundraiser finally came and Steve, Cooper, and I got dressed up in our fancy clothes. I'm a sucker for a theme party, but this was even better than Halloween.

From the moment we walked in, Cooper was a fan favorite. We shared a table with a wonderful couple and their dog who Cooper had worked with in the past. When it was time to go through the buffet line, Steve and I decided taking turns was best. The further we kept him from the buffet, the safer we were. As I went to get my food, I walked right by the "Doggie Buffet Line." How cute is that? There were four large bowls filled with people food for the dogs: Mashed Potatoes, Rice, beef, and bread. Wow, this was Cooper's lucky day! I obviously stopped to fill up a dog bowl full of each item and took it back to Cooper. When I set it down, before devouring everything, I do believe he actually paused, for a very brief second, as if to ask me if this was okay. They even had photographers onsite to document the fabulous evening.

Cooper was doing so well with his school visits that we also volunteered to participate as a "Rein-Dog" at our friend, Kimberly's, local charity annual Christmas Party for "Hope Junior." For several years, our family had selected a child to purchase gifts for, but this was the first time Cooper got to join in on the fun. Madison recruited a couple of friends to join us as elves, and we all had the best time. The kids were so excited to see and get to meet Cooper. We planned to read holiday books to the kids, but not much of that happened. The kids could not get enough of Cooper, it was adorable. There was one little girl who came back three or four times and would sit down and read one of the books to Cooper over and over.

What really happened

SO, THIS IS WHERE THEY GO

Journal entries 2018-2019

I FINALLY know what happens when the kids leave every day for 8 hours. This school thing isn't so bad. I go into a classroom, lie down on a rug, and get a parade of kids giving me one-on-one attention for a full hour while they read to me. Have I shared that I get treats before and after for being good?

This is also a whole new bonding experience for Mom and me. We have the best time with the kids, and I think she does appreciate me. She also enjoys sharing many of my stories with the kids.

Now, as for the dog fundraiser—that was so incredible, you can't make this stuff up! How many dogs get to brag about getting to go to a black-tie fundraiser? I must say, this was my best night ever. Okay, the black-tie was over-rated; so incredibly uncomfortable. I couldn't believe it when we walked in and they had photographers and water bowls everywhere. There were so many dogs to see, and those without dogs were all dog lovers, so I got plenty of attention. I already thought the whole thing was amazing, but then I saw the Doggie Buffet—REALLY! Finally, someone in this universe understands me. It also wasn't only me who was excited. I just know that Mom could not wait to take me that night.

CHAPTER TWENTY-EIGHT

BAD THINGS COME IN THREES

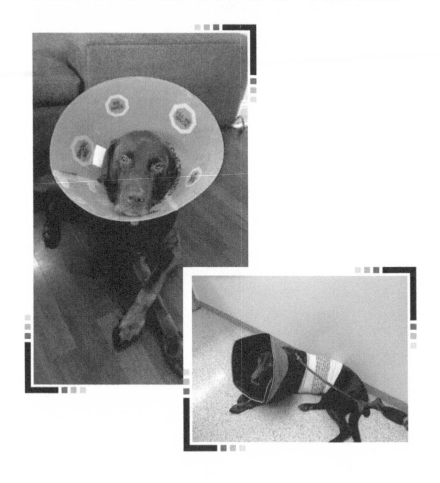

"When it rains it pours." After December 2018, I believe in this slogan more than ever. It all started in November when we decided to have a growth removed from Cooper's eye that was not going away and starting to impede his eyesight. Stand-alone, this wouldn't have been so bad. After a simple surgery one morning, he came home that evening with a cone to wear for two weeks. The worst part about these two weeks was on walks. Cooper would endlessly try to rip the cone off when walking by bushes. He would literally insert his head directly into the bush, then pull it to the side, hoping to catch it on a branch and rip it off. Not surprisingly, he got pretty good at it and soon was able to remove the cone on his own using regular household items. So, the two-week cone recovery turned into one-week.

He recovered just in time for the Christmas party season. I was preparing to host my annual ladies' holiday party, and Madison was making treats for her various Secret Santa gifts. We had four dozen brownies and several dozen Christmas cookies tucked safely in our Invisible Fence kitchen. I left to run some errands and left Cooper upstairs, thinking his collar would keep him out. I was distracted with the upcoming party and forgot that we still hadn't put his collar back on after his eye surgery because it wouldn't fit around his neck while he was wearing the cone. I returned a couple of hours later to an empty kitchen and many empty plates scattered around the house. Four dozen brownies and a couple of dozen chocolate cookies—GONE. I was actually worried this time, and immediately called the vet. I felt like the worst parent ever, getting scolded by the vet thinking I had purposely given the treats to our dog. She instructed me how to get him to throw up the chocolate by giving him a small dose of hydrogen peroxide. We attempted this a few times with no success. After all, he does have the stomach that can tolerate three pizzas and the Easter ham in one sitting. Soon after, Steve was on his way with Cooper to the emergency vet for a stomach pump and charcoal treatment. A long time and several hundred dollars later, Steve returned with one sick puppy. I actually felt sorry for him. I had never seen him so miserable. It took several days for Cooper get to himself after that excessive indulgence.

Fast-forward one week, Cooper was lying on the floor being pampered by Madison when she noticed a lump on his side. She immediately called me over. I have no idea how we had missed this coming on. It was about the size of an apple protruding out of his side, and it was now starting to bother him. He was picking at it, pulling the surrounding hair out, which now made it very visible. This time, I was terrified. I immediately put the cone back on him and scheduled a vet appointment for first thing the next morning. As always, my mind went directly to the worst-case scenario when we walked into the vet. My friend, Google, didn't help matters either. There is scary information out there on the web. One would think I should have broken up with Google after misleading me about the "dog-proof food container." I could tell that the vet shared my sentiments upon her initial examination. She then went to draw some fluid out of the growth in an attempt to get some answers. A look of relief immediately washed over her face. It was simply an infection abscess and it would ultimately drain on its own. No one is quite sure how he got it, but we were instructed on how to care for it once it drained. It sounded simple, but this quickly turned into a fiasco and turned us into frequent fliers at the animal hospital for the next month. The infection continued to grow, then ruptured, creating a large gaping hole in his side. This was followed by many bandaging attempts, and ultimately another surgery to suture his skin together. The only good news was that, instead of another month of cone punishment during this recovery, Cooper just had to wear a big t-shirt tied so that he couldn't get to his wound. Being a huge Cubs fan, he alternated between two oversized Cubs t-shirts we had.

Thankfully, he is now fully recovered, and this is all now just a bad memory. I felt so bad for him during this entire time. He was so miserable, and for the first time in his life, most of the pain he was feeling was no fault of his own. I was terrified we were going to lose him.

What really happened

WELL, THAT WAS RUFF

Journal entries December 2018 and January 2019

It's been a ruff few months! First of all, I had this thing on my eye that they decided to have taken off in surgery. This ticked me off because it wasn't bothering me. Then I heard them talking about me wearing the cone of shame for two whole weeks. It was awful and so humiliating. All of my friends laughed at me on my walks. I knew I had to find a way to turn those two weeks into one. I would oblige the humans for just one week.

Then came the brownie episode. Yes, I ate them, but who needs four dozen brownies and cookies in the kitchen? It was another one of those things that, once I started, I just couldn't stop. They were delicious. For the first time in my life, I will actually admit—I ate too much. Now I understand why they say that dogs should not eat chocolate. Whatever they did to me at the ER was terrible! It didn't even make me feel any better. How could that much brown fluid come from one dog? That was the worst food coma I've ever had.

Lastly, the infection was the absolute worst. It was so painful, and I didn't even do anything to cause it. Except maybe rubbing up against the fence—that might've given me a splinter. But OUCH! Luckily, they took the cone off only to replace it with an embarrassing shirt for three weeks. At least it was blue, and sometimes I got to wear one of Dad's Cubs shirts. Embarrassing, but better than the cone of shame and much better than the pink bandages I had to wear at the beginning. At least now I'm feeling better and am hoping to be back to my normal mischievous self in a week or two. Who knows what tales I'll have to tell you this year? There's so much more mischief just waiting for me.

CHAPTER TWENTY-NINE

TIMES ARE CHANGING

There have been quite a few changes around the house recently. John, the best dog sitter ever, who had watched Cooper since he was a puppy, could no longer watch him because he was battling a serious health condition. We all miss John and pray that he recovers soon. John's illness also meant that we had to find a new dog sitter. One might think that would not be a big deal. Cooper is so sweet and lovable; but remember, we're talking about an eating machine who can't be trusted. Friends weren't exactly lining up at my door for the chance to have Cooper stay at their house and ruin their cabinets.

We started using an app service called Rover. It seemed to be working pretty well, and after a couple of tries, we found a lovely woman, Ellie, who typically watches several dogs. Cooper seemed to get along with the other dogs. Ellie had watched him probably four times over several months. The first time at pickup, she shared that Cooper dumped over their large garbage can by the garage. He then led his new friends out back to enjoy a late-night garbage snack. The second time, he ate all of another dog's food; the third, he stole all of their buns for a BBQ. I concluded that I needed to either find another option or stop asking if he behaved. After all, she did keep agreeing to watch him, so she must like him. The final straw was on his last visit. I walked in to drop him off, and the first thing I noticed was twenty cases of "World's Finest Chocolate" bars that were stacked neatly on a table right inside the door. I quickly did the math in my head—twenty cases, twenty bars per case at $1.00 each. That is $400 I'm going to owe this woman when I pick him up, not to mention the vet bills to pump his stomach. All of this went through my head in about thirty seconds.

I must've been staring because Ellie said, "He won't bother these will he?"

"YES, he will!" I exclaimed loudly. "He'll eat them ALL. Is there someplace I can help you move them?"

She said, "Oh no, I'll have my son move them when he gets home."

I mumbled to myself "This isn't good, this is NOT good," as I walked back to the car. Time to find another dog care option. Luckily for all of us, Ellie moved the chocolate bars, and we averted a catastrophe. I also managed to find Brooks Canine, a wonderful dog boarding and training facility where Cooper gets to lounge in the comfort of the home of the owners who train dogs for a living and know how to handle most of his tricks.

The other big change around our household was that Madison recently left for college at Washington University in St Louis. This was a very difficult time for me to watch my oldest head to college. In retrospect, however, it was the year leading up to drop-off that was the most difficult. I would unexpectedly break into tears at the most inopportune times, such as at Madison's eighteen-year-old doctor's appointment. I cried to her pediatrician after she made the mistake of asking where Madison was going to school. Not to be outdone, another time I cried when Coach Downing, Madison's cross country and track coach for four years, asked me if the last track banquet felt a little different. Each of these occurrences truly horrified Madison while Steve looked on silently, afraid to say or do anything. Then there was Alex's reaction. I came home and told him I cried at the Track Banquet. He replied with a typical Alex response: "Mom, you know you still have one at home."

After my actions over the past twelve months, I think we were all terrified of college drop-off. This was going to be rough. Surprisingly, I was very proud of my behavior. Sure, there were the periodic teary-eyed moments, but for the most part, I held it together. Two months in, and Madison appears to be thriving and very happy. Not surprisingly, I'm not the only one who misses her. Every morning when I open up our bedroom door, Cooper walks in her room to look for her and then puts his head down and walks out when he realizes she isn't there. We try to get him to FaceTime with us, but he just doesn't get it and doesn't react to her voice at all over the phone. As an alternative, Alex and I do get him all excited now and then when we ask him where Madison is. We video his reaction and then send it to Madison.

What really happened

HELP – MADISON IS MISSING!

Journal entries 2019

I do not like these changes one little bit. First, I lose my vacation buddy, John. I miss him so much and wish I could listen to his songs and enjoy our long walks together. It's just not the same anymore when the family goes on trips. Now,

I have to go to a stranger's house and adapt to new situations. Although, whoever said that "You can't teach an old dog, new tricks" is seriously mistaken. I was so proud of myself for getting into the large garbage can at Ellie's. It was too tall for me to perform my highly perfected "jump and grab" routine. Instead, I had to push it up against the garage, gain some leverage, and then knock the whole can over. It took me a little while but, with multiple dogs onsite, for once—all eyes were not on me. Afterward, all of the dogs loved me for teaching them some new tricks. Don't get me wrong, I enjoyed Ellie's house. She is very sweet, and usually had many friends there for me to play with. I love my friends. Well, most friends. Every once in a while, there was a little chihuahua who barked NON-STOP. He was so annoying and loud, constantly pestering me. It got really old after about five minutes, and I had many more days of this "yap yap" crap.

Another benefit of Ellie's is that she does not know about all of my tricks. I'm usually able to grab some decent snacks. It's just too bad she can't keep her mouth shut, because she always tells Mom. Funny though, I think Mom is beginning to appreciate me because I'm not getting into nearly as much trouble. This last time, I almost won the lottery when I walked in and saw the chocolate bars. I could barely contain my excitement. This wasn't even going to be a challenge. Unfortunately, Mom saw it too and warned Ellie that keeping them there was not a wise move. After thinking about it, however, I kind of agree with Mom. I still have nightmares from the stomach pumping episode. I love chocolate, but I don't trust myself to stop after one or two cases.

The absolute worst change is that **Madison is missing, and no one even seems to care!** How can they not notice? I just knew that all of those suitcases in the front of the house in mid-August was not a good thing. Every morning, I walk into her room, and it's empty. I don't understand. I hear her name frequently and wait for her to run in and hug me, but nothing. I'm so sad. I really think I might be depressed. Every once in a while, they all look and talk into that phone, trying to get me to pay attention, but I'm just not a fan of technology. It only seems to distract everyone from more important things—namely me.

CHAPTER THIRTY

AH-HA MOMENT

As I was entrenched in writing this book, I often wondered how it would end. On several occasions, I thought I had found my last chapter. Yet new material that I could not ignore always soon followed, such as "The Case of the Missing Cliff Bars," "Cooper Goes to School," and "Bad Things comes in Threes."

One day, recently, as I was reflecting on the ending, it hit me. Despite our very rocky beginning after we first took him home, and all of our ups and downs over the years, our relationship has come completely full circle!

Reminiscing back to the day I first saw his massive brown blockhead and endearing eyes, he'd immediately stolen my heart. No question, he was the one I had to have! My mind then moves to the endless challenges he has presented over the years: ruined cabinets, mangled crates, stolen food, and pee on my bed. I had actually Googled locations I could send him for intensive rehabilitative training. Reluctantly, I must also admit that more than once, I silently asked myself if we should keep him. Then, right when his behavior was at its worst, I would always remember that Cooper saved Steve on that sunny November morning. Especially over the past two years, our connection deepened and became truly special once we started going to school together. I can't imagine life without him.

Early on, despite a love/hate relationship between Cooper and me, it was apparent to everyone that I was clearly his favorite. The kids get so mad because he has always come to me first. Throughout the day and at night, he follows me around nonstop. He won't ever go upstairs to bed until I do. Lately, I have been the first to head upstairs to bed, and he's always quick to follow. I've heard that dogs take on the personality of their owner but, holy cow, this is mind-blowing. How did it take me ten years to see these similarities? No respect for moderation, social gene, determination, loyal—check, check, check, check. I finally realized Cooper is me, in dog form—it was truly an Ah-Ha Moment!

Let's be honest, like Cooper, I'm not exactly known for my moderation. Although I have never eaten three pizzas in one sitting, I have been known to not necessarily follow the recommended portion size. There is also a chance that, on more than one occasion, I may have indulged in a little more wine than I should have, and possibly exhibited some behavior that I'm not exactly proud of. Just ask my friends who had the pleasure of watching me ride a mechanical bull in Nashville on my 50th birthday.

We both definitely inherited the social gene. This one hit me on our walk recently as Cooper peed on every passing tree, leaving me to stop suddenly in my tracks. OMG—this must be how Steve and the kids feel every time we're out and I run into my friends. They must be thinking, "Mom, can we please keep going? Do you have to talk to absolutely everyone?" When I shared this observation with Alex, his response was, "No, Mom, you're way worse than Cooper."

By this point in the book, we are all well aware of Cooper's strong sense of determination and ability to get things done. Once again, the traits I share. On my end, I will frequently step into volunteer for something. Before I know it, I'm the club president trying to find the best way to raise the most money for our cause.

That brings me to school. Cooper and I are both very loyal, caring, and love going together to read with the kids. There is nothing better than seeing the huge smiles on the faces of all the kids when we walk into the room. Watching the kids let down their guard and begin reading while their confidence soars is the best feeling ever. Cooper's excitement and howling when I grab his blue work bandana is pretty sweet too.

I've always said that Fitzroy is my favorite, but I must confess this question now actually requires some deep thought and reflection on my part. If I'm being honest, I guess I'd equate it to the saying that you never forget your first love. Fitzroy will always be my first and he will be "Forever in our Hearts," just like our sign says. Over the past few years, though, Cooper and I have truly connected. We really understand each other and have a mutual respect for our sometimes-suspect behaviors. I don't know if I'm ready to call him my favorite, but I also can't say that he's not.

What really happened

FINALLY

FINALLY, she gets it.

ACKNOWLEDGMENTS

First and foremost, I would like to give a huge thank you to Cooper for providing me with endless ups and downs, countless stories, and of course love throughout the past eleven years. Cooper and I would also like to jointly thank and acknowledge the many people who have fallen victim to his prey to help make this book a reality.

Thank you to the Caulkins family for breeding Lacy and making this journey possible. It's also been nice to swap sibling dog stories throughout the years with Julia Simone and the Kilburg family.

To Mary Beth Golden, thank you for giving me "the idea" and for being one of those people in life you are destined to meet and be friends with. You have also had to clean-up more than one of his garbage meals, so we appreciate those efforts.

I am so grateful to have the best friends a girl could ask for. This group of people encouraged me over the years to write this book, provided feedback, and are always so much fun to be around—Ellen Rourke, Kim Wambach, Molly Dietlin, Lora Winton, Susanne Strotman, Karen Rutili, Kathy Marino, Kate Lewis, Jen Myer, Jen Rabito, Anita Paxhia, Beth Harms, Diane Scully, Beth Barker, Lara Miller, Danielle Hartung, Leah Wolfe, Sherri Almgren, Erica Abdala, Mary Dow, Gina Gianikos, Gayle Mountcastle, Dede Kern, Michelle Tuft, April & Jeremy Armer, Jill Purcell, Kristin Nipke, and Amy Bergseth. A special shout out goes to Molly Dietlin for giving me the idea to name each of Cooper's chapters and suggesting the "two sides to every story" quote; Jen Rabito for her friendship and for finding us the "perfect" house, even if it *does* have a haunted basement; Sherri Almgren for providing me content for the baggage claim chapter; and finally, to my non-local Facebook friends for always asking when the book will be coming out and keeping me on my toes to share the latest escapades.

They say you can't pick your family, but I wouldn't trade mine for anything. Thank you to Lynn, John, Andrew, and Ethan Gripp for inviting Cooper into your home for three pizzas and the Easter ham. To Eric, Shari, Emily, and Hannah Johnson for not being upset when Cooper ate your bagels before the Thanksgiving Turkey Trot. To my amazing Mom, Beverly Hollenback, for always watching the kids in the early years and for giving Cooper snacks for anything and everything. To my Dad, Charlie Johnson, for teaching me early on that "Adventures are the best way to Learn." To Karen, Paul, Caitlin, and Connor Freitas for your ongoing encouragement, love, and annual stories we create whenever you visit. Caitlin Freitas gets special acknowledgement for always egging me on with my suggestions, even if they aren't necessarily the best ideas at times!

I am so appreciative of our Michigan neighbors for many reasons. Gloria & Alan Vandam, Charlie & (the late, great) Sue Edwards for listening to Cooper howl endlessly from the dock while we enjoyed our boat rides. The Gundy family for being understanding when Cooper would wander over and steal a snack out of your garbage can. The Novakoski family for alerting me and saving Cooper during his dangerous lake mission. Lastly, Jerry and Sandy Draheim, friends from our daily walks, who are never without a special treat for Cooper.

Thank you to our Michigan guests who throughout the years have enjoyed a front row seat to many adventures: Owen & Jimmy Rourke, for not having a clue how to fish and for helping Alex leave salami on the lily pad; the Scully family, for helping me craft our tubing experience and for watching Cooper when no one else would; Erica Abdala, for sharing your blueberry bread with Cooper; Lindsi Bradbury, for being another of those friends you are destined to meet, *even if it was a swim camp.* I'm sorry Cooper ate your Wheetabix. To the Paxhia family—Anita for the endless supply of wine; Tina, for sharing your birthday cake with Cooper; Allison, for being Cooper's first cheeseburger victim; and Joe, for the many things he's probably taken from you during your visits to Michigan. To Beth & Katy Harms—Beth for taking Cooper paddle boarding, and Katy for being understanding when Cooper destroyed your Vera Bradley bag in the days before he mastered his fine motor skills. To the Poppinga family for being such dog lovers, and especially Phil for being Coopers biggest fan.

Thank you to Pat K. for saving Steve (& Cooper) on that terrifying November morning. Thank you also for walking Madison and Alex to the bus stop.

A huge thank you to John Michaels for being the best dog watcher and devoted caretaker for both Fitzroy and Cooper throughout the years. We continue to pray for you.

It would have been hard for Cooper and my relationship to come full circle without the entire SitStayRead Organization. Volunteering for this wonderful organization filled a gap in my heart and fulfilled Cooper's lifelong dream of going to school. I would encourage all Chicagoland dog lovers out there to look into volunteering with them.

I can't forget to thank Google for always providing me with the answers to my frequently asked questions, and Culver's for being the most dog friendly fast food restaurant around. Acknowledgments couldn't possibly be complete without thanking the great folks at Northwest Animal Hospital for their compassionate and loving care of Cooper

As a first-time author, I am eternally grateful for all of the editing support that I received from old and new friends. To Lisa Railsback, my life long grade school friend and author, who was first to read my words and offer me insight and encouragement. To my dear friend, Diane Scully, for volunteering to be my second reader and for your meticulous attention to detail. Lastly, to Marni MacRae, the Best Fiverr editor I could have ever hoped for. I followed my gut in selecting you based on your enthusiasm. It paid off, and I feel like a gained a friend along the way. I would highly recommend your editing services to anyone.

Most of all, thank you to my family for listening to me talk about writing this book for years and for giving your ongoing love, support and encouragement after realizing it was really going to happen! This bucket list item is now complete, and I'm on to my next item... To Steve, for having the courage to perform a detail read through and edit even while knowing I'm not always exactly "receptive" to all of your ideas. Madison, for being the biggest dog lover on the planet and for your critical but constructive feedback that ensured I didn't embarrass you. Last, but not least, to Alex for always listening to me share my ideas and for giving me a healthy dose of perspective that brought me back to reality. I love you all more than words can say.

Made in the USA
Monee, IL
01 November 2020